Forgive, Release
and Be Free!

Forgive, Release and Be Free!

Joff Day

Sovereign World

Sovereign World Ltd
PO Box 777
Tonbridge
Kent TN11 0ZS
England

ISBN 1 85240 218 0

The publishers aim to produce books which will help to extend and build up
the Kingdom of God. We do not necessarily agree with every view expressed
by the author, or with every interpretation of Scripture expressed. We expect
each reader to make his/her judgement in the light of their own
understanding of God's Word and in an attitude of Christian love and
fellowship.

Cover design by CCD, www.ccdgroup.co.uk
Typeset by CRB Associates, Reepham, Norfolk
Printed in the United States of America

Contents

Acknowledgements

If you had seen the original version of this book, you could have read the cover like this: 'Settled Accounts – Learning How To Forgive and Release Joff Day'. This would usually bring a few laughs when I held up a copy to recommend it at meetings where I was speaking. People would ask, 'What on earth have you done to need to write a book instructing people how to forgive you?!' The truth is that probably everyone who has ever got to know me has, at some time, had to forgive and release me! But isn't that true of you too?

Firstly, I want to thank my wonderful wife Elaine and my children, Kate, Amy, Luke and Joel for their patient endurance towards a husband and dad who is trying to live what he preaches. As you can imagine, we have had plenty of opportunities at home to outwork the principles in this book! The rough and tumble of school, work and church have given plenty more. I have seen the grace of God at work in their lives as they have chosen to forgive and seen the character of God formed in them as a result. They are a constant joy to me!

Secondly, I am grateful to the mob in Cornwall we call 'church'! They have given me the opportunity not only to write this and share some of their stories, but also to teach it elsewhere whenever I can. Their willingness to live this message, as well as their encouragement and support, have meant more to me than they know.

I also want to acknowledge the help of my friends who read through the original manuscript and have offered corrections and suggestions. Their continuing belief in the principles and the practice of forgiveness, and their personal encouragement to me through the tough times, has been worth its weight in gold.

Special thanks for their encouragement to; David and Meryl Stanley; Nic and Jenny Harding and everyone at Frontline; Victor and Silvia Lorenzo – thank you for being obedient and moving to England.

Thanks too, to Sovereign World in taking the risk of publishing a book from a nobody from nowhere!

Foreword

In my hunger to know God, and go forward, I'm always looking for books that will help me along the way. In Joff Day's, *Forgive, Release and Be Free!* I have found another such book.

The body of Christ across the globe desperately needs this message. We all know from God's Word that we need to exercise forgiveness, but because we don't really understand the subject we enter into subtle deception in which we think we have forgiven people, while in reality we have not.

This unique book, written from years of experience, is the kind of spiritual dynamite that blows a hole in the deception of unreality that so easily lingers in our hearts.

Let's be sure we are not just readers, but distributors of this vital needed book.

George Verwer
Operation Mobilisation

What Others Have Said About This Book

Forgiveness is such a simple concept, why have a book about it? Primarily because the distance from concept to reality can feel like a chasm. After many years of Christian life and service I thought I understood forgiveness pretty well – I had even spoken on the subject! Then, like so many others, I experienced the decimation of some close personal friendships. Faced with intense feelings of betrayal I realised my previous understanding was impotent to help me forgive. Through the straightforward but life-changing message in this book I not only saw the gaping holes in my 'theology' of forgiveness but more importantly managed to cross the chasm of unforgiveness – some of those who I doubted I could ever speak to again are now among my closest friends and partners in ministry.

John Gibson
Singer/Songwriter

Just two weeks ago, travelling around the UK on a national seminar tour for marketing professionals, I spent hours speaking to a young man about the need for forgiveness. I have done this countless times in my life and on every occasion the material I instinctively use comes from Joff Day's book. It has never failed to help. In fact in my own travels, at any time and in any part of the world, I often come across people in need of freedom from unforgiveness. There is only one book I point them to – *Forgive Release and Be Free!* It has been a blessing and a release to scores of my contacts. I encourage pastors to keep copies in stock and ready for use.

David Oliver
Author of *Work: Prison or Place of Destiny* and
co-author of *Church That Works*

Joff offers keen insight into the practical application of the truth of biblical forgiveness. As John Wimber offered the body of Christ a practical model for healing prayer, Joff has created a practical model for ministering forgiveness. My wife and I had the unique opportunity of spending several weeks with Joff and the folks he works with, learning to forgive and release. It was nothing less than life-changing. We in turn have ministered it to others, who glow with the results of being free from bitterness, anger and resentment.

Michael Mathias
Businessman

Joff's book carries a life-changing message which, sadly, too many fail to apply. What kind of a world would we live in and how many doctors' waiting rooms would be emptied if we outworked on our lives the principle of forgive and release? Read the book and recover your health!

Dave and Chris Richards
Salt & Light Ministries

We found *Forgive, Release and Be Free!* to be an important book as it takes those who respond to its message into an experience beyond what is normally taught on forgiveness. Full release and freedom within has been experienced by those who have acted upon its message. We heartily recommend the book.

Don and Heather Double
Good News Crusade

This book has revolutionised the way we minister to people in the church. Most people who need help in a discipleship or pastoral context have forgiveness issues to deal with. Joff's book has virtually become required reading for church members and is a set text in many of our training programmes.

Nic Harding
Frontline

Forgive, Release and Be Free! is one of the handful of books that we encourage every member of our congregation to read. Its message is absolutely fundamental to embracing the freedom that Jesus wants for every Christian. There are very few who are not impacted and blessed by Joff's clear and insightful teaching.

David Stanley
Heartlands Church

Introduction

Why forgive and release? I am using these two words to convey one biblical concept – forgiveness. Jesus taught clearly that to forgive is also to release.

Sadly, there are many Christians who do not understand this. Some have been taught by well-meaning leaders that even though they may have forgiven someone for an issue, if they are still hurting they will have to forgive that person again and again (for the same issue) until the hurt finally disappears.

If Jesus' teaching on forgiveness was to be understood correctly, such a person has probably not forgiven 'from their heart' in the first place. They may have made a mental decision to 'forgive', but their heart has not 'released' the offender from the debt. That may well be why they still hurt concerning the issue.

There is much hurt and mistrust in the body of Christ today. Some of it lingers on because the principles of forgiveness have not been fully understood. This book seeks to explain forgiveness, not to create a 'forgiveness plus ...' gospel.

For many people I have spoken to, understanding forgiveness as 'forgiving and releasing', has helped them put an end to many unresolved hurts from their past, and come into a new freedom in Christ. It has also helped them make a commitment, for the future, to forgive as Jesus taught, whatever circumstances come their way.

Some people may choose not to read a book on forgiveness because their understanding or their pain has already biased their thinking away from the it. I would like to start by saying what forgiveness isn't.

Forgiveness is not:

- Excusing or condoning a wrong. It is not saying the wrong that someone did is now OK.
- Putting the past behind us. It is not overlooking or ignoring an offence. One writer said, 'Forgiveness begins not in forgetting, but in remembering.'
- Reversing or cancelling the consequences of wrongs done. There are many in physical prisons today who may have found the forgiveness of God or been forgiven by their victims. But they still have to live with the consequences of their actions.
- The same as reconciliation. There can be no reconciliation without forgiveness, but reconciliation may or may not result from forgiveness.
- Suppressing our feelings. Forgiveness of deep hurts may require the expression of deeply suppressed emotion.
- Something that 'weak' people do. People who forgive are strong.
- Always a single event. It is often a process that may take time to work through.

If you have ever had cause to forgive anyone or think you may need to now or in the future, then this book is for you.

Chapter 1

A Wounded Heart

When I looked at the wound on the top of my leg, my stomach turned. There was a gaping hole, exposing weeping infected flesh. The wound was about eight inches long and the edges were red and inflamed. God then spoke to me.

'If you will forgive and release Sue (not her real name), then I will heal the wound.' The question I had was 'After what she's done, how can I?' I felt I was owed. I had given what I thought a steady relationship like ours required. I really did love her. I thought I had done everything to be faithful to her, but now she had jilted me, with no real explanation. I was hurt and disappointed.

She had been on fire for God once. There were times when I had been totally intimidated by her boldness and confidence. Recently her walk with God had grown cold. A move in her job had given her a new start and the opportunity to make new friends. It also gave her the chance to finish with me and go out with someone else she had found.

Now every time I thought of her I felt sick in the pit of my stomach. When I heard people talking about her or mentioning her name, I winced. When I saw her it was worse! As the weeks went on, the pain did not decrease. The old adage 'Time is a good healer' seemed to be a load of rubbish. Now God was asking me to forgive her.

It was Capel Bible Week. One speaker had told us to go and get things sorted out where relationships were wrong in our lives. It was a beautiful hot summer's day so I went into a marquee to pray. As I started to pray I had a vision (or some form of picture) of the top of my leg. I was wearing shorts, so the picture seemed vivid and real. In the vision I saw a wound on my leg. I could easily see how it was like the wound I felt in my heart. Then the Lord showed me that whenever I thought about this person I had loved, the devil took a knife and dug it into the flesh. The pain was excruciating, the sense of unfairness overwhelming.

I could bear it no longer. I forgave her and released her from all that I sensed she owed me. I also asked God to forgive me for being bitter, jealous and judgemental. As I did this, I saw a hand come down over the wound on my leg. As it passed over the top of my leg, the wound vanished.

'What do you see?' came the voice again. 'New flesh', I replied. 'Touch it', the voice said. I touched my leg. There was no pain, but it was sensitive to touch. 'There is no scar. Your emotions are whole again, and you can be hurt again.' At that moment, I knew that I had settled accounts that had been outstanding. God had graciously forgiven me too, and inexplicably brought healing to my heart.

When I saw or spoke to Sue after that, I couldn't believe how I felt. No anger, no jealousy, no resentment. It was wonderful.

Chapter 2

Roots, Fruit, Seeds and Soil

About ten years later, while meditating on the issues of forgiveness, God started to teach me afresh what really had happened to me in that marquee at Capel. He showed me another picture, which, I trust, will help you settle accounts once and for all with those who have hurt you.

Your experience may be like mine in that most people you meet who constantly grumble, complain, gossip or speak negatively are usually hurting on the inside. Now there are several things that happen when a person has been hurt. One is that they continually mull over the situation in their mind and let the hurt get worse. The problem is that the more the conscious mind rehearses the offence or offences, the more the unconscious mind gets infected with the poison of unforgiveness.

Another thing that happens is that they try to bury the hurt. Then defence mechanisms build up on the inside, both mentally and emotionally. These negative thought patterns (strongholds) promise to protect a person from getting hurt again. For example, 'I'll never get involved with a woman again.' 'He let me down badly. I'll never do business with his sort again.' Rationally these defences make sense. But that which is built up to defend, quickly becomes a stronghold that imprisons.

Another option is revenge! They decide to deal with the people who have hurt them by hurting them back. And, if they are really hurt, they then try to hurt the offender before the offender gets a chance to hurt them again! This way of thinking becomes a stronghold that can appear to provide 'safe' distance from others. Sometimes in marriages that are struggling one partner will try to hurt the other because they don't want to get hurt themselves.

However, the bottom line with all these options is that on the inside a person becomes bitter. God's heart is that we don't get bitter, we get better! That is the Christian option. You don't stay hurt, you get healed. The writer to the Hebrews says this:

> *'See to it that no one comes short of the grace of God; that no root of bitterness springing up causes trouble, and by it many be defiled.'*   (Hebrews 12:15)

So the root of bitterness:

- springs up
- causes trouble, and
- defiles many

But it also causes someone to come short of the grace of God. The grace of God has been described as the 'undeserved favour of God'. What might be the implications of coming short of God's undeserved favour? We are going to look at this in more detail, later in the book.

A root doesn't usually just start life as a root. The Bible has a lot to say about roots, fruit, seeds and soil. As the picture in Figure 1 develops, we will see how we get hurt emotionally and the effect it can have in our lives.

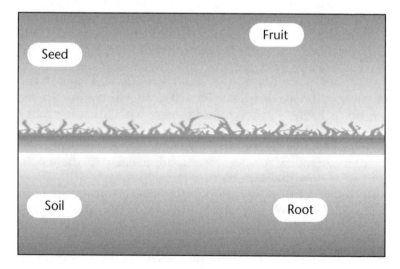

Figure 1

We will also see that as a result of the soil of insecurity within our lives, seeds of offence take root and bear poisonous fruit. Mental, emotional and physical sicknesses and afflictions are often the result. However, the good news is that God has provided a way to 'reverse the curse', dig out the roots and provide us with internal security. But first we need to understand the principles of forgiveness.

Chapter 3

Debts and Debtors

Matthew 5 – 7 has been rightly described as the 'Manifesto of the Kingdom'. Here, Jesus spells out practically what life is like for citizens of the kingdom of God. Living under the government of God, with Jesus as King has implications.

> 'Pray, then, in this way:
> "Our Father who is in heaven,
> Hallowed be Your name.
> Your kingdom come.
> Your will be done,
> On earth as it is in heaven.
> Give us this day our daily bread.
> And forgive us our debts, as we also have forgiven our debtors.
> And do not lead us into temptation, but deliver us from evil.
> [For Yours is the kingdom and the power and the glory
> forever. Amen.]"
> For if you forgive others for their transgressions, your heavenly
> Father will also forgive you. But if you do not forgive others, then
> your Father will not forgive your transgressions.'
>
> (Matthew 6:9–15)

The sense behind the word debt is 'that which is legally due'. The sense behind the word 'debtor' is 'one that has not yet made amends to one whom he has injured'. The NIV renders Matthew 6:14–15 as follows:

> 'For if you forgive men when they sin against you, your heavenly
> Father will also forgive you. But if you do not forgive men their
> sins, your Father will not forgive your sins.'

Jesus makes it very clear in these verses that if we don't forgive, then God will not forgive us. And He is talking about life under the new covenant, not the old. This is confusing for some Christians. They say, 'Oh but when I got saved all my sins were forgiven.' Look at Luke 11:4, where Jesus, some two years later, reiterates to His disciples how to pray:

> *'And forgive us our sins,*
> *For we ourselves also forgive everyone who is indebted to us.*
> *And lead us not into temptation.'*

There are several Greek words translated 'sin'. The word 'sins', here, is the Greek word *hamartia*. It has the sense of 'failing to reach the mark'.

God has set His standard for our lives. It has been spelt out as the Law. Jesus said the whole of the Law and the Prophets could be summed up in two commandments:

> *'And he answered, "YOU SHALL LOVE THE LORD YOUR GOD WITH ALL*
> *YOUR HEART, AND WITH ALL YOUR SOUL, AND WITH ALL YOUR STRENGTH,*
> *AND WITH ALL YOUR MIND; AND YOUR NEIGHBOR AS YOURSELF." '*
> (Luke 10:27)

When we fail to meet these standards, we sin. Someone commented that if these are the two greatest commandments, then the greatest sin must be in not obeying them. So what is our debt to God? Our debt to God is that we owe Him a life of heartfelt love as well as demonstrating that love by loving our neighbour as ourself. This is why there is not one person on the planet who does not need the forgiveness of God. God's forgiveness and salvation are only available through a personal faith in Jesus Christ.

We too, inwardly, have standards of how we feel others should treat us. Usually these are fair and reasonable. But when people fail to reach the mark we have set, we sense that there is a debt outstanding. According to Jesus, that debt needs to be dealt with.

> *'If we confess our sins, He is faithful and righteous to forgive us*
> *our sins and to cleanse us from all unrighteousness.'*
> (1 John 1:9)

There are big implications in these verses. If we refuse to forgive those who have offended (are indebted to) us, we still have sin in our heart. Why? Because the Lord has not forgiven us because we will not forgive. If we have sin in our heart there is no cleansing and no righteousness.

In Luke 6 Jesus gave more practical teaching about handling hurt and conflict:

> *'But love your enemies, and do good, and lend, expecting nothing in return; and your reward will be great, and you will be sons of the Most High; for He Himself is kind to ungrateful and evil men. Be merciful, just as your Father is merciful. Do not judge, and you will not be judged; and do not condemn, and you will not be condemned; pardon, and you will be pardoned.'*   (Luke 6:35–37)

'Pardon' in the last verse is the Greek word *apoluo*. The New International Version translates it 'forgive'. It literally means 'release'. We could therefore accurately render the last part of this verse: 'Release and you will be released'. What is the context of this verse? It's to do with how you contend with those who hurt you. It's about forgiving them. And not only forgiving them, but releasing them.

Now read the next verse.

> *'Give, and it will be given to you; They will pour into your lap a good measure – pressed down, shaken together, and running over. For by your standard of measure it will be measured to you in return.'*   (Luke 6:38)

I had always thought that this verse was to do with money. I have heard it quoted many times when offerings have been taken! The principle here can probably apply to money as well, but money isn't the context. From reading the previous verses, the context is to do with forgiving and releasing.

So what do we give here? Surely forgiveness. What will be given to us? Forgiveness in 'a good measure, pressed down, shaken together running over, they will pour into your lap. For by your standard of measure it will be measured to you in return' (Luke 6:38).

Jesus is saying that if you want to be forgiven, you yourself must forgive. If you want to be released, you must release those who have hurt you and those who have mistreated you. If you give forgiveness, then God's forgiveness can be poured out on you. It's the principle of sowing and reaping. If you sow unforgiveness, what are you going to reap? If you sow forgiveness what are you going to reap?

Looking for the breakthrough

Many Christians live with unforgiveness in their heart and wonder why they can never get the 'breakthrough' in God they are looking for. They wonder why they never move in power. They wonder why they rarely move in spiritual gifts. They've tried everything. They've listened to every tape from 'men of faith'. They've read every book for 'overcomers'. They've been to Bible weeks, conferences and conventions, yet they still can't break through.

They may well argue that their 'position' and 'identity' in Christ means that they don't need any more forgiveness than the complete forgiveness they received when they were first saved. However, there is a good probability that there is still unforgiveness in their heart; and unforgiveness that they may not have 'connected' with. Maybe you are one of those people. Right now you may be thinking that you don't have unforgiveness in your heart and that you are not owed in any way. If you are open to the Holy Spirit, why not pray now and let God show you as you read on:

> 'Father, please will You show me if I have any areas of unforgiveness in my heart. I do not want to cover anything up. Please show me where I have claimed that things are "under the blood", when in reality I have just swept them "under the carpet".'

Chapter 4

The Unforgiving Servant

In Matthew 18, Jesus tells a parable to explain what He has just said to Peter about forgiveness. The parable is about settling accounts and is pretty much the definitive teaching of Jesus concerning forgiveness. Some of us, when we think about the people that have hurt us, would like to settle our accounts by doing to them what they did to us! But first, let us read the conversation between Peter and Jesus in Matthew 18:

> 'Then Peter came and said to Him, "Lord, how often shall my brother sin against me and I forgive him? Up to seven times?" Jesus said to him, "I do not say to you, up to seven times, but up to seventy times seven." ' (Matthew 18:21–22)

Jesus was not saying forgive the person 490 times, then on the 491st time take revenge! He was saying forgiveness has no limitations. Nor was He saying that when you think of a person who has wronged you, forgive them, and if you think about it again, forgive them again for the same issue. Some Christians believe that constantly 'forgiving' someone for the same issue will gradually take the pain away. It doesn't. Accounts have to be settled.

Look at 1 Corinthians 13:5:

> '[Love] does not act unbecomingly; it does not seek its own, is not provoked, does not take into account a wrong suffered.'

The New English Bible says:

> 'Love keeps no score of wrongs.' (1 Corinthians 13:5)

Some people imagine that God has an index card in heaven with their name on it, recording all the wrongs they do. When they sin and come to God, it seems that God digs out their index card. When they confess what they have done, God looks at the card and says, 'That's the sixth time you've done that this week. We had better put this one down as well.' He then 'lets them off' because they have confessed their sin.

God does not behave like that! He forgives us and releases us. Even if He were to pull out our imaginary card, He would say, 'Your card is clear. There's no record of any wrong here. You are sorry for your sin? I forgive you.' As a result, according to 1 John 1:9, we would receive His righteousness and cleansing.

The parable that follows makes clear that if you properly forgive a person who wrongs you, the next time it happens it is as if it were the first time. You don't keep count. True forgiveness does not count how many wrongs have been done against us.

Look what Jesus said in Luke 17:

> *'Be on your guard! If your brother sins, rebuke him; and if he repents, forgive him. And if he sins against you seven times a day, and returns to you seven times, saying, "I repent," forgive him.'*
> (Luke 17:3–4)

What was the disciples' response to this?

> *'Increase our faith!'*   (Luke 17:5)

What Jesus said is not a mandate for being a doormat as a Christian. Neither is it a mandate for being an abusive Christian! He gives clear instructions about dealing with wayward Christians. We will pick up on them later in the book. Let's read the parable Jesus told in full.

> *'For this reason the kingdom of heaven may be compared to a king who wished to settle accounts with his slaves. When he had begun to settle them, one who owed him ten thousand talents was brought to him. But since he did not have the means to repay, his lord commanded him to be sold, along with his wife and children and all that he had, and repayment to be made. So the slave fell to the ground and prostrated himself before him, saying, "Have patience with me, and I will repay you everything." And the lord of that slave felt compassion and released him and forgave him*

the debt. But that slave went out and found one of his fellow slaves who owed him a hundred denarii; and he seized him and began to choke him, saying, "Pay back what you owe." So his fellow slave fell to the ground and began to plead with him, saying, "Have patience with me and I will repay you." But he was unwilling and went and threw him in prison until he should pay back what was owed. So when his fellow slaves saw what had happened, they were deeply grieved and came and reported to their lord all that had happened. Then summoning him, his lord said to him, "You wicked slave, I forgave you all that debt because you pleaded with me. Should you not also have had mercy on your fellow slave, in the same way that I had mercy on you?" And his lord, moved with anger, handed him over to the torturers until he should repay all that was owed him. My heavenly Father will also do the same to you, if each of you does not forgive his brother from your heart.' (Matthew 18:23–35)

Notice some of the phrases. You might want to highlight them in your Bible:

- This parable is about *settling accounts.*
- One man *owed* the king, but couldn't pay.
- The king felt compassion for him.
- The king released him.
- The king forgave him the debt.
- The forgiven slave found a fellow slave and said *pay back what you owe.*
- When that slave asked for mercy *he was unwilling.*
- He threw his fellow slave in prison until he *paid back what was owed.*
- The king, angered by what he heard, said, 'Should you not also have had mercy on your fellow slave?'
- Because of the slave's lack of mercy and unforgiveness the king *handed him over to the torturers* until *he should repay all that was owed him.*

A contemporary parallel

Let's make the parable contemporary and personal. A bank manager desires to sort out those customers who are in arrears. You have a £100,000 mortgage and are five months behind with your payments, due to unemployment. The interest rate has just increased again. He invites you in for an interview to find out how you are going to pay the arrears. You really have no explanation. He then tells you the bad news that your house is to be repossessed, and your possessions sold until the repayment is made. You break down in front of him, begging for more time.

This bank manager feels great compassion for you, knowing that you will never be able to pay, even if you get a job. He then says to you that he will personally clear the arrears and the outstanding mortgage in totality. In addition, he will clear your overdraft, credit cards, car loan and settle any hire purchase arrangements you have, leaving you debt free.

You leave his office a financially free man. Next day at McDonalds you meet a man who owes you £50 for a repair job you did to his car three months ago. He's promised to pay you for ages, and still doesn't have the money. Angered, you take him to court to recover the debt.

One of his friends knows the manager of the bank and at lunch with him one day, tells him what happened. You get another call from the bank for another interview. This time he's the angry one. 'I said I would personally pay your debt, because you asked me for leniency. Why weren't you lenient with your debtor, as I was with you?' He then rescinds his previous decision. He sends you to court to have the repossession order carried out. You are bankrupted and left on the street penniless.

The analogy ends here. Bankrupts are not sent to prison and in modern prisons torture is not allowed!

A debt too big to repay

The king knew the servant couldn't pay back what he owed. Remember that this parable is teaching truth about our relationship with God and with others. We are the servant that owed the king ten thousand talents. There is no way that we can pay back to God what we owe Him as a result of our sin. We call to God for mercy when we become a Christian. We ask Him to forgive us.

Forgiveness alone is not enough

The king felt compassion, released the man and forgave him the debt. You see 'forgiveness', as many people understand it, was *not enough* for this man. It was not enough for the king to say to him, 'I forgive you *for the fact that you owe me this money.*' Being given another thirty days to pay would not have helped. Ten thousand talents was probably far greater than the Gross National Product of Palestine in Jesus' day. If the king had just 'forgiven' him, the man would have known there was still an outstanding debt. The king could still have said at any time, 'You still owe me. Pay up!' For the man to experience *true forgiveness*, he needed releasing from the debt.

Forgiveness must be received

The forgiven servant went out and met someone who owed him. But when was he owed the 100 denarii? Before he was forgiven by the king or after he was forgiven and released by the king? From the text it seems that he was owed before the king forgave him.

Before going on to points four and five, what are some of the implications of the last point for us? One preacher suggested that the reason this man wanted his 100 denarii was so that he could start to pay the king back, despite what the king had done for him. As a result of not fully accepting the king's mercy and forgiveness, his conscience was not clear. He thought he would start to pay back what he owed anyway, however insignificant the amount may have seemed.

The implication for us is that if we do not fully receive God's forgiveness at an emotional level, we can start to act in a way that we think 'pays God back'. We can get into all kinds of religious rigmarole and legalism in trying to gain God's acceptance. Some of this may include good Christian practice like Bible reading and prayer. But if we are doing these out of a sense of guilt coming from a bad conscience, they are, what the Bible calls, dead works. The writer to the Hebrews says:

> *'For if the blood of goats and bulls and the ashes of a heifer sprinkling those who have been defiled sanctify for the cleansing of the flesh, how much more will the blood of Christ, who through the eternal Spirit offered Himself without blemish to God, cleanse your conscience from dead works to serve the living God?'*
>
> (Hebrews 9:13–14)

Many Christians sentence themselves to a life of 'doing time' trying to pay God back because they have not or cannot fully accept the forgiveness of God. The blood of Jesus is the only thing that can cleanse our conscience. Hebrews 6:1 says dead works are something we should have repented from!

We must also face the fact that there are people who have offended us and things that have happened to us before we became Christians. These things may have wounded us, making us feel we are owed. Those things did not necessarily get resolved just because we became Christians. Some would like to believe that when they became Christians everything became brand new. They quote verses like the following:

> *'Therefore if anyone is in Christ, he is a new creature; the old things passed away; behold, new things have come.'*
>
> (2 Corinthians 5:17)

But when we become Christians, not *everything* becomes new. When I say that, I am not trying to contradict Scripture! Let's be honest, our bank manager did not write off our mortgage at the good news of our salvation. Had we been through three divorces, we would not be instantly reconciled to all three wives! If you became a Christian while in prison, you couldn't just walk free the next day. You still had to pay the penalty of your wrong-doing. There were many things that impacted our lives before we became Christians, and those things can still affect us now.

Many people, particularly in evangelical churches, have been told that when they became Christians, all of their past was dealt with. They have been told that their past has no effect on them anymore. Unfortunately that kind of theology lacks integrity. The terrorist who maims and murders one day, yet repents the next, is surely not released from the responsibility of his actions, is he? His salvation will not bring back to the bereaved families their loved ones. He must still face the consequences of his actions.

No, the new creation is to do with our *spirit*. We are body, soul and spirit. When we were born again, our spirit was renewed (Titus 3:5). On the day of resurrection we will get a new body (1 Corinthians 15:50–53). Meanwhile, God wants to sort out our personality – our thoughts, decisions and feelings – what we call our 'soul'.

Our spirit is regenerated by the working of the Holy Spirit. Our ability to know God intimately is changed by rebirth. Our conscience is cleansed and sharpened. We are given a new ability to worship the Creator as 'Daddy', not just as 'Almighty God, Maker of Heaven and Earth'. Our body certainly does not take on immortality at conversion! We must await the resurrection for that. The truth is that there is still much that needs changing in us. The work yet to be done is primarily in our mind, will and emotions, which have been damaged through sin and its effects. Right now God is still working in us to change us.

Consider these verses:

> *'For I am confident of this very thing, that He who began a good work in you will perfect it until the day of Christ Jesus.'*
>
> (Philippians 1:6)

> *'So then, my beloved, just as you have always obeyed, not as in my presence only, but now much more in my absence, work out your salvation with fear and trembling.'* (Philippians 2:12)

> *'Therefore I urge you, brethren, by the mercies of God, to present your bodies a living and holy sacrifice, acceptable to God, which is your spiritual service of worship. And do not be conformed to this world, but be transformed by the renewing of your mind, so that you may prove what the will of God is, that which is good and acceptable and perfect.'* (Romans 12:1–2)

> *'But we all, with unveiled face, beholding as in a mirror the glory of the Lord, are being transformed into the same image from glory to glory, just as from the Lord, the Spirit.'*
>
> (2 Corinthians 3:18)

However, the following verse teaches us that right now we are as righteous as God is:

> *'He made Him who knew no sin to be sin on our behalf, so that we might become the righteousness of God in Him.'*
>
> (2 Corinthians 5:21)

If, in Christ, I am the righteousness of God, what happens when I sin? Do I need to ask for forgiveness? Why do I need forgiveness if I'm righteous? Theologians can answer this question by explaining the difference between our 'standing' and our 'state' before God.

Our standing is what Christ has made us in eternal terms. Our state is how we are practically right now. If a beggar who lives on the street is left £50 million in a rich person's will, his standing is one of tremendous fortune. His state may be that he currently lives in a cardboard box, has holes in his shoes and is broke. There are things that are going to have to change if he is to fully inherit his inheritance!

The same is true for us. Our spiritual inheritance is wonderful, but there is action that we need to take to appropriate it. The gospel we have believed has to be worked out practically, not just acknowledged theoretically. In Ephesians Paul writes:

> *'Therefore, laying aside falsehood,* SPEAK TRUTH EACH ONE *of you,* WITH HIS NEIGHBOR, *for we are members of one another.* BE ANGRY, AND *yet* DO NOT SIN; *do not let the sun go down on your anger, and do not give the devil an opportunity. He who steals must steal no longer; but rather he must labor, performing with his own hands what is good, so that he will have something to share with one who has need. Let no unwholesome word proceed from your mouth, but only such a word as is good for edification according to the need of the moment, so that it will give grace to those who hear. Do not grieve the Holy Spirit of God, by whom you were sealed for the day of redemption. Let all bitterness and wrath and anger and clamor and slander be put away from you, along with all malice. Be kind to one another, tender-hearted, forgiving each other, just as God in Christ also has forgiven you.'*
>
> (Ephesians 4:25–32)

This does not all happen automatically overnight! The Holy Spirit is continually working within us to change our character into the likeness of Jesus.

Now let's return to the parable in Matthew 18.

Forgiving others

The servant did not have mercy on his fellow servant by forgiving and releasing him. It is implied from the king's reply that he was expected to do so, *because* the king had forgiven and released him.

There are practical implications for us here. This parable does not make sense if it only refers to debts that lie in the future. Jesus is clearly implying that there may be debts outstanding in our lives from our pre-Christian past. Do we let people who 'owe' us from our past stay locked up in a prison in our heart, bringing them out occasionally for a quick beating? Or are we going to open the account books of our emotions and start to settle accounts?

The prison of unforgiveness

The unforgiving servant was handed to the torturers to extract every last penny that he owed the king. We should forgive because we have been forgiven. If we don't, not only will the Father not forgive us, He will hand us over to the torturers! This statement will be a bit mind boggling to some Christians. It seems to go against everything they think they understand about God's unconditional love! Torture and the love of God are totally incompatible aren't they? Yet Jesus promises that the Father will do the same to us if we do not forgive from our heart. We will see the implication of this later.

You could pray the following:

> 'Father, please show me if in any way I am like the unforgiving servant. Show me if I have only accepted Your forgiveness with my mind and not my emotions. Show me where I have rationalised my hurt and show me the people that I need to forgive.'

Chapter 5

The Soil of Insecurity

Let's look at the picture in Figure 1 again (Figure 2).

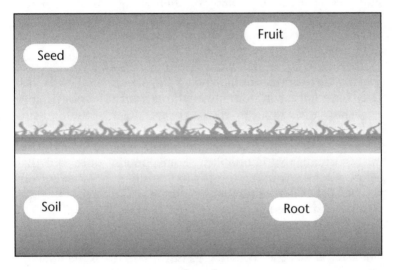

Figure 2

When God first showed me this picture, He told me to draw it for people when I was helping them to forgive others, so that they could see the process involved.

When we have a truly secure relationship with somebody, we can usually say anything without causing or receiving offence from them. For example, I have a good friend called Dave and he will occasionally come out with a question like, 'Joff, how is it that you are so incredibly ugly and I am so incredibly good looking?' Now you might think that this is either a very unfriendly thing to say or a very funny thing to say – it could depend on whether you have ever seen me or not!

Now because I know Dave well (and suspect that someone may also have said the same thing to him in the past!) I do not take offence or feel rejected. I enjoy the friendly banter, asking him if he wants help to reach the light switch. (Actually, he's not that vertically challenged!)

But what if a total stranger said the same thing? That could be a totally different matter! I could be very hurt. (In fact, with four children and friends like Dave, I am very secure about my physical appearance!)

There are times when friends who are close to me need to come and tell me the truth about myself, that they know will hurt. The Bible calls it *'speaking the truth in love'* (Ephesians 4:15). Their words cut me, not to expose me and leave me emotionally bleeding, but so that things that need to change in me (which I can't usually see for myself) can be dealt with.

These are the 'faithful' wounds of Proverbs 27:6 which come into my life to bring healing. There is no 'offence' in these words. They have not taken from me anything which did not need to go. I do not feel owed by them. I'm grateful that these friends accept and love me enough to come and tell me my faults.

Someone once said, 'Love without truth is sentimentality and truth without love is brutality.' Someone else once said that before you take your ten ton truck of 'truth' to another person, you had better make sure there is more than a matchstick bridge of relationship and security between you. If you don't, great damage and offence can be caused.

In the parable of the sower in Mark 4, Jesus mentions different kinds of soil that the Word of God is sown in. It was the soil type that determined the growth. For a seed to take root effectively, there had to be fertile soil. The soil is, of course, referring to the hearts of the listeners.

The fundamental reason we have been hurt in the past, and are liable to get hurt in the future is this – we have the soil of insecurity in our heart (see Figure 3).

Divine purpose

God's intention is that the soil of our hearts is to be tended and nurtured primarily by our father and mother in the early years

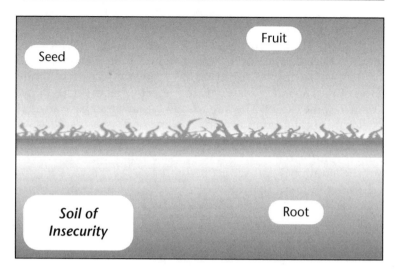

Figure 3

of our development. The home should be a place of love, appreciation, acceptance, affection and encouragement. As our personality (mind, will and emotions) develops, the correct balance of love and discipline produces security within us.

If good seed, consisting not only of actions but words of love, affirmation and encouragement, are sown, then in time the fruit of that will be evident in our lives. The good seed will produce a harvest of those positive attributes that we can give to others. The fruit of the Spirit (Galatians 5) will flourish in abundance. If we have the soil of security within us, when seeds of offence or hurt come, we can deal with them constructively.

But if the soil in our heart is the soil of insecurity resulting from a less than perfect (dysfunctional) family background, two things happen. First, any good seed that is sown finds difficulty taking root. The soil may be shallow, full of stones and rocks. It may have thorns and thistles growing that choke out the good seed. Second, the soil of insecurity provides a fertile ground for the seeds of hurts and disappointments to take root quickly.

I was once speaking at a men's meeting and painted a verbal picture of a child growing up in a loving home where there was always plenty of encouragement and acceptance as well as loving discipline. The child developed a healthy self-image and personality. I asked a question, 'How many of you think this child will never feel rejected in their teenage years?' No hands went up. 'How many think that despite their upbringing, this teenager may feel rejected and hurt by their parents?' Every hand went up.

I have yet to meet anyone that has come from a perfect family background! Sociologists tell us that most families are dysfunctional to some extent. The implication is that we all have areas of insecurity and rejection within us. None of us is as secure as we think we are! The problem is that we have got used to rationalising the hurts that come our way. As a result, we don't ever sort out the emotional damage properly.

Now let's look at the seed.

Chapter 6

The Seed of Offence

A root usually starts as a seed that has been planted. I want to call the things that hurt us the seeds of offence. Let's look at the picture again (Figure 4).

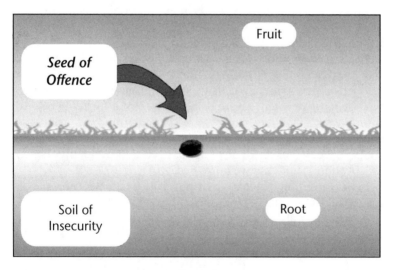

Figure 4

There are seeds of offence that are sown into the insecure soil of our lives, producing a harvest after their own kind. The seeds germinate and produce a root as well as fruit. There are four basic ways that those seeds of offence get sown into us.

What others have said to us

Some people grow up constantly being told, 'You're useless', 'You're no good', 'You'll never amount to anything', 'You're just like your father … a loser', 'You're a failure'. Some people are told, 'You're ugly', 'You're fat', 'You smell', 'You've got fleas', or called 'Rabbit ears'.

To cope with the humiliation, we were reminded to sing the little rhyme: 'Sticks and stones may break my bones but names will never hurt me.' That rhyme is a lie from the pit of hell! As a kid I said it and tried to believe it, but the names still hurt! I would have preferred a few sticks and stones! I knew cuts and bruises on my legs got better. The feelings that went with being called names never seemed to.

Today school bullies are using mobile phones, text messages and email to harass other pupils. In 2000, the British charity ChildLine, a telephone helpline for children, spoke to more than 22,000 children about bullying. Over half the calls were from children whose lives were being made miserable as a result of verbal, rather than physical bullying. Some children were so traumatised that they spoke of feeling suicidal.

You see names hurt. Names wound. Always being reminded of our weaknesses and failings hurts us. Do you know what happens when someone calls us stupid, useless, or a failure? As well as being rejected, we are being robbed! We are being robbed of self-worth. We are being robbed of dignity. We are being robbed of a sense of value. How do I know that? Because we are made to feel less as result of what has been said. Suddenly there is a debt there. Suddenly we feel owed.

If we get enough negative things said to us, we can end up losing all self-respect. Not only do we hate those who have offended us, but we end up hating ourselves. We look in the mirror and say the same things we have heard. We speak to ourselves and say 'You're ugly … I hate you!' I have counselled both teenagers and adults who told me that they have sat in front of a mirror speaking hate and curses to themselves.

What others have not said to us

Think of all the encouragement you needed as a kid, but didn't get. As I said earlier, God's plan for mothers and fathers is that they encourage their children, build them up, bless them, and speak good things into them. But how many times have we missed hearing, 'Son I think you're great ... I really love you.' 'Darling, it really doesn't matter that you failed your maths exam. I still think you're wonderful!' Some of us missed that kind of unconditional love and acceptance. We were brought up to understand that love is performance based. If we did well we felt accepted. If we didn't make the grade, we felt rejected.

What was worse however, was when we thought we had done well and deserved praise, yet it didn't come. What wasn't said to us hurt as much as the negative things that had been spoken to us. It hurt deep down on the inside. It hurt when someone did as well as we did and was congratulated, yet no one said anything to us. As a result we feel robbed. We feel owed those words of encouragement that never came. We feel owed the words of approval that never came.

The Scripture records two occasions when God rolled back the clouds of heaven and spoke of His Son. The first was at His baptism, when He spoke to Jesus personally.

> ' ... *and the Holy Spirit descended upon him in bodily form like a dove. And a voice came from heaven: "You are my Son, whom I love; with you I am well pleased."*' (Luke 3:22 NIV)

It seems that even Jesus needed to hear words of approval from His Father. God was, in effect saying, 'I love you Son, I think you're great.' If Jesus needed to hear the words, how much more should we?

The second occasion was at Jesus' transfiguration. Here, God spoke to those who were with Jesus.

> '*While he was still speaking, a bright cloud enveloped them, and a voice from the cloud said, "This is my Son, whom I love; with him I am well pleased. Listen to him!"*' (Matthew 17:5 NIV)

Fathers should not only give personal approval and affirmation to their sons. They should also be prepared to speak well of their sons when others are around. How many can think back to the days when we were put down in front of others by those who should have been building us up. As a result we felt robbed. We feel owed.

Many dozens of people I have spoken to have said the same thing: 'I suppose my dad told me he loved me, but I don't ever remember it.' 'I suppose my mum must have said she loved me loads of times, but I just can't recall one.' There's an ache in their hearts. There's a void in their hearts where they feel owed those words of love and acceptance.

What others did to us

Today the newspapers and TV documentaries give us constant reminders that we live in a society permeated by abuse. Domestic and marital violence, sexual and child abuse are all on the increase. In reality, these increases may only be apparent because people are becoming more honest about what is actually going on. Ninety-five per cent of sexual abusers of children are men. Many surveys show that most abusers were abused themselves.

Recently there have been reports on young people who have committed suicide due to constant bullying at school. Any kind of physical abuse leaves you feeling owed; it leaves you feeling robbed. Some people who read this book will have been sexually abused. For some, the only way to deal with the pain and anguish caused by the abuse is to bury the issue. Pretend it didn't happen. But all that really happens is that a lid gets put on the 'sewer' within. I use the word sewer because the potent mix of shame, guilt, condemnation, regret, anger and unforgiveness can feel like an emotional sewer.

When a person is abused sexually, they have been robbed. Ask any single woman who has never had sex and then been raped. She's had her virginity ripped from her. She is owed. 'I know my father said he would never do it again, but he couldn't help it. He said himself that it's what his father did to him.' A woman who was sexually abused by her father may make excuses that satisfy her mind, but they don't reduce the pain within. If the woman who experienced that trauma becomes a Christian, everything does not necessarily become wonderful overnight. There can still be a lot of hurt, rejection and shame.

My mother was visiting my father who was in a London hospital for a minor operation. She had travelled on the train and was walking the last few yards to the hospital. Suddenly a young man ripped her handbag off her arm and dashed away into the crowd of people. She was thrown to the floor, powerless to do anything. Thankfully she was not physically hurt more than a few bruises. Her handbag contained money, credit cards and other personal possessions. The police told her there was little or no hope of recovering her bag, even though the thief was probably only interested in her cash.

It's obvious she felt owed financially. But the situation is more subtle than that. She was robbed of time; contacting the police, ringing round to cancel credit cards, writing to confirm details. She was robbed of her sense of security and peace ... this happened in broad daylight on a busy street. The thief would have been able to get her address from the contents of the bag and maybe he would plan to burgle her house. Could she make him repay what he owed?

You may think that none of this applies to you. You may have had a reasonably trauma-free life. But it's not just major traumas that can leave you feeling owed. What about the careless driver who scraped the paint off your car door in the car park and just left a slip of paper on your windscreen saying, 'Sorry Pal!' Doesn't he owe you? How are you going to make him pay? What about the time when a careless child ran past you in the playground and ripped your new school dress. You were the one who got blamed by your parents, despite your protests. You can still feel owed years later ... even if you've become a Christian.

What others didn't do

This is probably the biggest one of the four. Unfulfilled expectations. Disappointments. 'If you pass your exams, then daddy will buy you that mountain bike you've seen in the shop in town.' Expectation in you rises sky high. You know that if you put the extra effort in you can pass. The results come through and you get straight As. But there's been a shake up at your father's firm and he loses his job. There is no redundancy pay. Dad is very apologetic. 'Son, I'm sorry, but we don't have the money to get you the bike.' In your mind you rationalise the situation. 'We've got no money, we can't afford a bike.' But your emotions are not rational. They tell you, 'I'm owed a bike. He promised me a bike.'

Years later you cannot understand why you get angry at small injustices in your life. The truth is that the feelings of injustice go right back to when you were owed the bike by your father. In fact, if you go back to the issue in your mind, you can still feel how you felt twenty years ago. The account is still outstanding in your emotions. You still feel owed. There's a debt that needs dealing with. Look at this proverb:

> *'Hope deferred makes the heart sick,*
> *But desire fulfilled is a tree of life.'*   (Proverbs 13:12)

It was Hannibal Smith from the TV series *The A Team* who said, 'I love it when a plan comes together!' We are all like that. Isn't it wonderful when your plans come together? It could be a romantic weekend away with your wife that you've been keeping secret for months. Or a special holiday abroad for the first time. Maybe the house you really wanted, but which had been sold, is back on the market at £5,000 less than you were prepared to pay. Desire fulfilled is a tree of life. When things go well, we want to go *'Yesss!'* like the little boy in the film *Home Alone*!

But what about a plan that hasn't worked out, that's gone wrong? It makes the heart sick. The word 'sick' means afflicted, ill, weak, faint and wounded. Many of us have had promises made to us that have been broken. The broken promises that hurt the most are by the authority figures in our lives. Primarily this means our parents but it also includes teachers and especially church leaders if you are a Christian. Church leaders unwittingly wound many of their flock by making promises they do not keep, or cannot keep. I know this because I have been guilty of it myself. They may promise to encourage, approve and affirm us, but rarely are they able to give us the time or input we feel we need.

Why do we get hurt by this? It is because we believe that what those authority figures say must be the truth. Not only that, they seem to have the power to fulfil what they have said. Again, it is so easy to rationalise it all and make excuses, 'Well it's not their fault, circumstances have changed.' But on the inside, at what we call gut level, it still hurts.

God's plan is to heal the hurts from the past. A major part of this is forgiving and releasing. When Jesus began His ministry He spelled out His commission this way:

'THE SPIRIT OF THE LORD IS UPON ME,
BECAUSE HE ANOINTED ME TO PREACH THE GOSPEL TO THE POOR.
HE HAS SENT ME TO PROCLAIM RELEASE TO THE CAPTIVES,
AND RECOVERY OF SIGHT TO THE BLIND,
TO SET FREE THOSE WHO ARE OPPRESSED,
TO PROCLAIM THE FAVORABLE YEAR OF THE LORD.'   (Luke 4:18–19)

The Living Bible says:

'... he has sent me to heal the brokenhearted and to announce that captives shall be released and the blind shall see, that the downtrodden shall be freed from their oppressors ...'
(Luke 4:18–19)

Part of this commission is to set free the downtrodden, to bind the brokenhearted. Does this mean the physical healing of the organ that pumps blood round our bodies? No. It's to do with healing damaged emotions. If hope deferred makes the heart sick, then Jesus is the person to come to for healing!

Why was the proclamation of the favourable year of the Lord good news to the poor? The favourable year of the Lord was the Year of Jubilee, which came round every fifty years. You can read about it in Leviticus 25. It was the year of cancelled debt. Whatever you owed another person was cancelled in that year. This meant that in every person's lifetime, there was the possibility of being free from debt. What a wonderful provision of God! How sad Israel never actually celebrated it.

Jesus' declaration of the Year of Jubilee here was a declaration of debt cancellation. However, this was primarily in the sense of cancelling people's 'sin debt' – the falling short of God's standards. The good news was and is that you can have your debt against God wiped out. You can be forgiven for your sin.

Consider some more reasons for there being outstanding debts in your life:

- physical illness or disease either personal or in a parent robs us of health and happiness
- physical or mental handicap
- trauma, e.g. war, imprisonment, the sudden death of a parent or close relation, divorce
- substance abuse, e.g. an alcoholic or drug dependent parent
- physical or sexual abuse

- religious bigotry or piety, e.g. children brought up in strict religious order, robbed of their personality
- adoption and fostering – did you get a good deal?
- family ambition and control – were you sacrificed on the altar of your father's ambition? For example, did you have no friends because you went to twelve different schools in fourteen years because of your father's promotion in his job? Children of missionaries and church leaders are also hurt for this reason.

All these can cause major hurt and disruption in the formative years of a person's life.

In our school and college years, subtle family control can result in frustration, anger and resentment in later life. Because we had to become something someone else wanted us to be, we can feel robbed of our own personality.

For example, did you have to carry your parent's Christian name? 'Hi! My name is John Dunkin. This is my son, John Dunkin Junior and his son will be John Dunkin III.'

Did you have to follow in the footsteps of a parent's career? 'Father, grandfather and great grandfather before him all went to the same college at Cambridge; so must you.'

'This family's military history is unique, son. *We* (you) must keep the family name in the Regiment.'

'We have a long nursing tradition in this family, dear. You wouldn't want to break it would you?'

'Every branch of this family has had someone enter the Anglican ministry. Now you wouldn't want to spoil things by becoming a non-conformist, would you?'

We often feel that there is no need to forgive that which is 'understandable' human frailty or shortcoming. The real question is though, *do we feel owed*? Often our real feelings have been rationalised in order to cope. Christian teaching on 'ruling' our thoughts and emotions has meant that we *control* the pain and disappointment of the past rather than *confront* it. Sadly, much ruling is fooling!

Having read the above list, you may now need to re-read this chapter, but without making excuses for those who 'owe' you. Ask God to let you get in touch with any feelings you have buried. You may find you have some debt cancelling to do! Maybe you could pray this:

'Heavenly Father, You know that I have tried to forgive. I have to admit that I still feel owed by some. I have tried to bury the hurt, but it is still there. Please show me everywhere I have forgiven at a mind level, but not from the heart.'

If you are not yet a Christian, and would like to be, go to Appendix A at the back of this book. When you know that you yourself have been forgiven and released by God, you will be able to forgive and release others beyond doubt.

Chapter 7

The Manure of Judgement

When the seed of offence starts to germinate, the judgements we make against those who have hurt us become the manure for the soil of insecurity, which in turn feeds the root of bitterness. In the Sermon on the Mount, right after Jesus speaks of seeking first the kingdom of God, He says:

> *'Do not judge so that you will not be judged. For in the way you judge, you will be judged; and by your standard of measure, it will be measured to you.'*   (Matthew 7:1–2)

Here is the principle of sowing and reaping again. Some while ago God started to speak to me about judging others. It was not a comfortable experience. I realised that I had been judging people left, right and centre! I remember walking into town one day and seeing one of the many 'travellers' we have in our part of the country. He had an extreme haircut and more piercings in just one of his ears than a classroom full of teenagers! His clothing was classic New Age. In addition he had a small dog with him (unemployed people get more social security payments if they own a dog). His whole demeanour was quite intimidating.

I found my internal defences working overtime. 'It's my tax that is paying him to keep a dog! It's my tax that has probably paid for his piercings and tattoos! Here he is, sponging off the state and he's not the only one ...' And so I went on. What a good job my thoughts were not written on my T-shirt! About 20 yards further on the Holy Spirit got hold of me. 'That's only your opinion. How would you like to be judged like you judged him?' came the question. 'You can't see his heart. You don't know his history. You don't know what I am doing in his life right now.

You don't even know whether he's an evangelist being culturally relevant!' Before I could internally mutter one line of argument, the Holy Spirit said, 'Repent you ugly thing!' (Yes. The Holy Spirit really does speak to me like that!) What else could I do?! So I started with the traveller and then thought of more than a few other incidences I needed to repent for as well.

There have been times when I have felt judged wrongly by others. Haven't you? The truth is that we may have just been reaping what we had sown at another time. We all tend to think that we are 'normal' and measure everyone else by our standard of normality. This can either make us proud that we are better than 'them', or jealous and intimidated and so we put ourselves down.

There is power in the words that we speak, and when internal judgements we have made are verbalised, they carry destructive power. We shall see more of this later when we look at the fruit of resentment. Jesus said:

> *'... For the mouth speaks out of that which fills the heart.'*
> (Matthew 12:34)

I think it is important to make a distinction here between a spoken comment that may be negative and a comment that is judgemental. I believe that Christians should have a positive confession and that we should:

> *'Let no unwholesome word proceed from your mouth, but only such a word as is good for edification according to the need of the moment, so that it may give grace to those who hear.'*
> (Ephesians 4:29)

However, some Christians do go a bit overboard on the postive confession thing. Some to the point where they trap themselves into a subtle form of legalism and inevitibilty that could lead to fatalism. 'Every word you speak is a seed that is sown. Once you have sown it, it will bear fruit,' they say. Well let's take the issue away from words ... to carrots. If I sow some carrot seeds, is it inevitable that carrots will grow? (Those who know my gardening skills, please don't answer!) The answer is: not necessarily. If I decide that really I wanted cabbages instead of carrots, I could dig the carrot seeds up. Even though I sowed carrots, they won't grow because I have dug the seeds up. Let's go back to the issue of words.

Suppose I have a conversation with someone and go away thinking that I am sure they have misunderstood me and that what I said came over too negatively. I do not have to think, 'Oh well, I can't do anything about that. What will be will be.' I can go back to them and tell them more clearly what I mean. 'Ah but the damage has been done!' I can hear someone saying. No it hasn't. I just went and dug up the seed. Of course, if the person has been offended, I can apologise and ask their forgiveness.

Those of us who are parents have probably said plenty of unhelpful things to our children when they were growing up – more than likely in the context of discipline. Suppose you just caught your young child painting all over your brand new dark green leather settee with a silver paint pen that you left lying around. It's possible that in your annoyance and anger you might say something like, 'You are a naughty boy! Look what you have done! Daddy is very cross indeed!' Now, did you just prophesy to your child? Did you curse them? Or did you just state a fact at that point in time? I don't honestly believe that you are saying, 'I prophesy to you that you are a naughty boy and you always will be, world without end!' You are also not saying, 'I curse you with the curse of being a naughty boy!' You are stating the facts as you see them at the time. It's probably still better to separate the child's behaviour from their identity and say something like, 'What you have done is very naughty! Daddy is very cross!' (Actually, I don't remember the exact words I said when I saw my son after he had painted our new settee!)

Some people would say that I am somewhat insightful. I can see issues in people's lives that may not be evident at a natural level. It is part of my gifting from the Holy Spirit. There are times when I see negative things and may state them as a fact. 'John. I believe you are covering up some sexual sin that you must confess.' Although the statement may appear to be negative, I am not judging him and condemning him for his sin. I am just stating what I see and giving him an opportunity to respond. However, if I know he is covering up some sexual sin and then I am harsh, severe, critical or condemning, I have crossed the line into judging him.

When Paul said, 'You foolish Galatians!' in Galatians 3, was he judging them? Or was he stating a fact, that to go back to observing the Law now that they had the Holy Spirit was, in fact, foolishness?

Luke's version of Jesus' statement on judging is:

> *'Do not judge, and you will not be judged; and do not condemn, and you will not be condemned; pardon, and you will be pardoned.'* (Luke 6:37)

Luke makes the connection between judgement and forgiveness. We looked at the meaning of the word 'pardon' earlier. Primarily Jesus was speaking to His disciples at this time, not to the Pharisees. Obviously He views the judging of others by His disciples as a serious issue that has serious consequences. Implicit too, is that the consequences of judgements we make in the here and now are suffered in the here and now – not one day in the bye and bye.

In the context of salvation, judgement and condemnation is past for the Christian. Jesus said,

> *'Truly, truly, I say to you, he who hears My word, and believes Him who sent Me, has eternal life, and does not come into judgment, but has passed out of death into life.'* (John 5:24)

The apostle Paul said,

> *'Therefore there is now no condemnation for those who are in Christ Jesus.'* (Romans 8:1)

So if we have passed out of judgement and condemnation, how can we still be judged by God now? Probably the most straightforward scripture to answer that question is in 1 Corinthians:

> *'But a man must examine himself, and in so doing he is to eat of the bread and drink of the cup. For he who eats and drinks, eats and drinks judgment to himself if he does not judge the body rightly. For this reason many among you are weak and sick, and a number sleep. But if we judged ourselves rightly, we would not be judged. But when we are judged, we are disciplined by the Lord so that we will not be condemned along with the world.'*
> (1 Corinthians 11:28–32)

Although the context is the Lord's supper, the principle is clear. When we judge others, we ourselves are judged by the Lord. When we are judged by the Lord, we are disciplined by Him. In Hebrews 12:6 the writer says the Lord disciplines those whom he loves. It also adds a few verses later that the discipline is sorrowful not joyful! If the discipline of God is sorrowful, it's probably going to be painful. Could this have physical as well as emotional consequences? In Corinth, it seems that some people were sick and some had died prematurely as a result of breaking bread with judgement in their hearts towards someone else. I don't believe God can give sickness to anyone, but might He lift His hand of physical protection from someone who is judging someone else? It appears so.

What are we doing when we judge others?

When we judge others we are, in effect, putting ourselves in the place of Jesus:

> *'because He has fixed a day in which He will judge the world in righteousness through a Man whom He has appointed, having furnished proof to all men by raising Him from the dead.'*
>
> (Acts 17:31)

Taking the place of God is called idolatry and comes from a proud heart! It was the reason Lucifer fell from his prominent position in heaven. It is also stupidity! God is the only person who really knows the hearts and thoughts of another person. The problem is that we deceive ourselves into believing that we can see into people's hearts and, therefore, have the right to become judge, jury and executioner. Someone once said, 'We tend to judge ourselves by our intentions and others by their actions.' Trying to do God's job for Him is not a good idea.

Sometimes we judge others out of our own fear and insecurity. We believe that we are right, our opinion about what happened is right and therefore our judgement is also right. The fact that someone hurt us means they must be in the wrong. Because we feel robbed or owed, judging them makes them smaller in our eyes and makes us feel better. We've evened the score. It makes us feel like we are back in control. But are we?

Francis Frangipane says that we should be prayermental not judgmental. In other words, rather than allowing the offences we suffer to turn to bitter judgements against others, we should pray for the offenders instead. This is a way of reversing the plan of the enemy. The opposite of accusation is intercession.

In the next chapter we will see how the judgements we make produce a bitter root that eventually takes control of our life.

Chapter 8

The Root of Bitterness

If no action is taken to remove the seed of offence, it quickly germinates. As we dig the manure of judgement into our soil of insecurity, two things happen. A root goes down and a shoot goes up. Let's look at how the picture is developing (Figure 5).

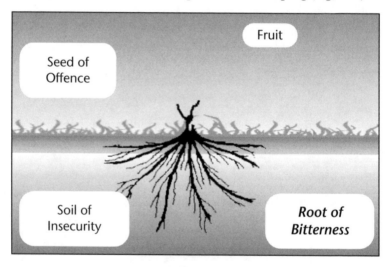

Figure 5

When you get hurt on the inside by any of the four seeds of offence, the first effect occurs under the surface. You can keep a smile on your face, 'It's OK Dad, don't worry about the bike.' But on the inside the reaction may be, 'You liar! ... I'll kill you one day.'

Can reactions be that extreme? I have talked to people who would have liked to murder their father because of what he did.

Sometimes it was because of what he didn't do, that they thought he should have done. That is how hurt and damaged they were. That kind of attitude spreads like cancer on the inside. It becomes a root of bitterness within.

> *'Wash your heart from evil, O Jerusalem,*
> *That you may be saved.*
> *How long will your wicked thoughts*
> *Lodge within you? ...*
> *"Your ways and your deeds*
> *Have brought these things to you.*
> *This is your evil. How bitter!*
> *How it has touched your heart!"*
> *My soul, my soul! I am in anguish! Oh, my heart!*
> *My heart is pounding in me;*
> *I cannot be silent,*
> *Because you have heard, O my soul,*
> *The sound of the trumpet,*
> *The alarm of war.'*   (Jeremiah 4:14, 18–19)

In these verses we can see the effect of sin on the emotions. Bitterness is linked with agony in the heart.

> *'But if you have bitter jealousy and selfish ambition in your heart,*
> *do not be arrogant and so lie against the truth. This wisdom is not*
> *that which comes down from above, but is earthly, natural,*
> *demonic. For where jealousy and selfish ambition exist, there is*
> *disorder and every evil thing.'*   (James 3:14–16)

If there is a root of bitterness in a person's life, sooner or later it will surface. The root of bitterness:

- is poison, it slowly eats away at you on the inside;
- causes anguish and pain in the heart;
- is associated with jealousy and selfish ambition – 'I'll show them';
- provides an entrance for demonic activity.

When it springs up (becoming external), it:

- causes trouble

- defiles many – to 'defile' means 'to contaminate' or 'to pollute'.

Bitterness works on the inside in the following two ways.

What you feel

When somebody hurts you, other than physically, the first place it gets you is not in the mind but in the pit of your stomach. Jesus had perfectly balanced emotions. However, He was not unfeeling when He saw the plight of others.

> *'And two blind men sitting by the road, hearing that Jesus was passing by, cried out, "Lord, have mercy on us, Son of David!" The crowd sternly told them to be quiet, but they cried out all the more, "Lord, Son of David, have mercy on us!" And Jesus stopped and called them, and said, "What do you want Me to do for you?" They said to Him, "Lord, we want our eyes to be opened." Moved with compassion, Jesus touched their eyes; and immediately they regained their sight and followed Him.'*
>
> (Matthew 20:30–34)

> *'I feel compassion for the people because they have remained with Me now three days and have nothing to eat.'*   (Mark 8:2)

The Greek word for compassion is almost unpronounceable unless you are Greek or a Greek scholar. It is *splagchnizomai*, pronounced 'splangkh-nid'-zom-ahee'. It means: 'to have the bowels yearn; to be moved in the inward parts; to be filled with tenderness'.

In Eastern culture the bowels were understood to be the seat of the emotions. In today's vernacular we would say that when Jesus heard the blind men's plea for help, it got Him in the guts. Remember Matthew 18? What was said of the slave's Lord when he saw the slave could not pay? *He was moved with compassion*. It's the same Greek word.

When we get hurt, when the seed of offence is sown, it gets us in the guts. It may hurt a lot or a little. If we do not confront it, the root goes down and the shoot springs up and ultimately bears the fruit of resentment. We can try to bury the issue but, possibly years later, we will suddenly hear a name that triggers off in us a torrent of hurt feelings. We wonder where it all came from. The truth is, it came from the emotional sewer we talked about earlier. We feel owed, we feel hurt, we feel bitter.

Bitterness can be experienced in varying degrees. Something can be so bitter to the taste that your tongue wants to crawl down your throat. Or bitterness can just be a bad taste left in the mouth. In fact when something unpleasant happens to us, we might even use the expression that 'It left a bitter taste in my mouth'. Sadly, some experiences that we have had both before and after our conversion have left a bad taste in our mouth. Here are some of the characteristic emotions that go with these experiences.

A sense of injustice

'It's not fair.' That's one of the biggest emotions to cope with when we have been hurt. In fact, it is the easiest way to know whether we are really hurting on the inside or not. If we do not feel we can change our circumstances, if we feel we are out of control, then we sense injustice. If we do not overcome it, then we feel frustrated.

Frustration

Frustration comes as a result of some hope, some aspiration, some action we take being thwarted. It also comes as a result of someone else thwarting our plans and hopes. If a root of bitterness is already at work in us, then the outworking of that frustration is anger. Good sense gets overruled by negative emotion. For example, suppose we get to the station in plenty of time to catch our train, which will get us to the airport with just enough time to catch our plane. At the time the train should leave it stays stationary at the platform. We look at our watch. Five minutes pass and we begin to get irritated and fidgety. Our worst suspicions about the rail company are being realised.

After ten minutes a guard comes through the carriage asking everyone to leave this train and go to one on platform 15, which is due to leave in two minutes. Our temperature is rising fast. It will take at least a minute to get off the train and find a luggage trolley. We finally blow up at the guard, 'Why can't you lot ever get it right?!'

The guard then explains that there has been a major derailment a mile further up the track, and it is thought that fifteen people may be dead as a result. All trains are being diverted. We respond with a grunt. We have a choice to make at this point. Do we let frustration become anger at how inconvenienced we have been? Do we start to sizzle like the proverbial pressure cooker? Or do we realise that the source of our inconvenience, the source of our frustrated plans is a mass of tangled metal and bodies where lives have been shattered and torn apart?

If there is no root of bitterness within, we will probably feel ashamed or embarrassed that we had so quickly pre-judged circumstances that we knew nothing about. We apologise to the guard and making our exit for the alternative train, we pray for the wounded and dying and their families. Patience is the opposite of frustration. It is a fruit of the Holy Spirit that enables us to persevere and endure.

If there is a root of bitterness within, our response could be somewhat different. We feel justified in our criticism of the rail company. After all, it was probably their fault the derailment happened. Not only that, if we miss that plane, they are going to pay for it. They will have to pay for another ticket, pay for our hotel accommodation and pay for the extra meals we will have to buy. We intend to *make them pay* for what they owe us.

Anger

The injustice does not have to have been suffered personally. One lady my wife and I were counselling had a continuous problem with anger. We asked about her childhood and found that her parents had adopted a boy when she was small. The father always treated the boy differently to the rest of the family. He was always harsher and more demanding on the boy than on the other children. As a child this lady had tried to protect her adopted brother, taking on herself all the unfairness with which he was treated. Years later, the boy had become a homosexual. As we were talking she suddenly saw that she felt great anger and resentment towards her father for the way he had treated her adopted brother. Until then, she had not realised the source of her anger. When she got angry either with her children or husband, it always seemed to be totally out of proportion to the preceding circumstances. When she confronted the hurt within, and forgave and released her father, great healing came into her life.

Anger is a natural consequence of frustration. Another example: trying to slacken a wheel nut on a car, the wheelbrace slips off resulting in a gashed knuckles on the gravel in the gutter. The motorist, in frustration, throws the wheelbrace at the ground, where it bounces back, hitting his shin with great force.

Who was to blame for this incident? Who is the motorist really angry at? The wheelbrace? The car? The mechanic who over-tightened the nut? Or himself for not taking more care? Anger is always an expression of emotion towards people, not towards things. More often than not intense anger is the venting of the hurts and injustices experienced in a person's past, whether recent or not.

Like a volcano, anger can be waiting to explode over some poor unsuspecting person. Somebody can come along and say something quite innocently, but the response is an eruption of hurt feelings within. It is as if someone came along and pricked a boil and the contents splattered out over anyone nearby. Hebrews 12:15 says the root of bitterness *springs up*. It is almost as if one minute it is not there, and the next minute it is. This kind of person ends up being harsh and judgemental like the elder brother in the parable of the lost son. He or she may become a perfectionist, demanding of themselves and others standards that cannot be met. Anger then becomes part of their character. When their 'kettle boils' anger is not just 4–5 on the Richter scale but has become a rage at around 8–9.

What is the answer? The answer is not to put another plaster on the boil. The answer is to sort out the boil, to drain the poison and infection out, to disinfect the wound, and for it to be healed.

Hatred

Anger, if not handled correctly, can easily become hatred.

'I hate my father for what he did. Even though he's dead, I hate him.' I have heard people say that. Their parents have been dead and buried long ago, but they still hate them. They still feel owed. Extreme anger becomes hatred. It becomes hatred of those who have offended or hurt them. They only have to think of the name of the person and their countenance changes. They can feel the venom within. But if the venom within is not removed, it will eat away and poison every part of that person's being. Like cancer, it will destroy them.

Some people shift their anger onto themselves. Hatred also gets turned onto themselves. They will scratch, bite and inflict pain on themselves. They will literally bang their head against a wall until it is bruised and bleeding. Why? Because *it's unfair*. Anger and hatred can be expressed verbally and physically. I call this the 'fruit of resentment'. It is the external manifestation of that which is within.

Violence is an expression of a sense of injustice felt deep within. Riots that we see flare up on housing estates happen as a result of years of tension which has built up inside the residents, particularly young people. For many it is the frustration at the injustice of being jobless. They feel owed by the firm that made them redundant; owed by the company that would not give them a job and owed by the government for seemingly doing nothing. Eventually the hurt, the anger and the hatred get taken out on people and property.

If anger and hatred are not expressed, they become suppressed: pushed down on the inside until they apparently disappear. But the result is often depression. Underneath most people's depression is unforgiveness towards others or themselves.

God's perspective on emotion

Anger is an emotion that is a part of every normal human being.

> '*BE ANGRY, AND yet DO NOT SIN; do not let the sun go down on your anger, and do not give the devil an opportunity.'*
> (Ephesians 4:26–27)

The context of these verses is to do with the rough and tumble of everyday life as a Christian. This scripture says that it is possible to be angry and not sin. It could also be read as an instruction to be angry. Why? Because anger is better expressed than suppressed. How many sermons have you ever heard on 'How to be angry in a godly way'? How many of us when we were growing up were taught how to express our anger in a healthy way?

The only way you can be angry and not sin is to express your anger in a healthy way and then forgive and release the person that made you angry. It is not something that should be left for a few days, a few months, or a few years. *'Do not let the sun go down'* means start today, do it now.

There are instances in the Bible, where God is angry.

'Now the LORD was angry with Solomon because his heart was turned away from the LORD, the God of Israel, who had appeared to him twice.' (1 Kings 11:9)

Even Jesus got angry. Having entered a synagogue, He came across a man with a withered hand. He then asked the Pharisees if was right to heal on the Sabbath.

'After looking around at them with anger, grieved at their hardness of heart, He said to the man, "Stretch out your hand." And he stretched it out, and his hand was restored.' (Mark 3:5)

But the Bible also tells us:

'For His anger is but for a moment,
His favor is for a lifetime;
Weeping may last for the night,
But a shout of joy comes in the morning.' (Psalm 30:5)

and

'But You, O Lord, are a God merciful and gracious,
Slow to anger and abundant in lovingkindness and truth.'
(Psalm 86:15)

God can also hate:

'For I, the LORD, love justice,
I hate robbery in the burnt offering.' (Isaiah 61:8)

Because of the unfaithfulness of Israel, He said:

'I hate, I reject your festivals,
Nor do I delight in your solemn assemblies ...
But let justice roll down like waters
And righteousness like an ever-flowing stream.'
(Amos 5:21, 24)

Psalm 45 speaks prophetically of the Lord Jesus:

You have loved righteousness and hated wickedness;
Therefore God, Your God, has anointed You
With the oil of joy above Your fellows.' (Psalm 45:7)

So we see that it is possible to be angry and to hate without sin, provided that the subjects of our anger and hate are the same as God's. In Ephesians Paul says,

> *'... for when you are angry, you give a mighty foothold to the devil.'*   (Ephesians 4:27, Living Bible)

Footholds quickly become strongholds. What was once a propensity to anger can become an almost uncontrollable reflex. Why would anger give a mighty foothold to the devil? Anger is a product of unforgiveness. Holding unforgiveness in your heart is effectively a rejection of Jesus' sacrifice on the cross. Demons therefore, can not only easily gain access to people through their unforgiveness but will also 'turbo-charge' their negative emotions. If forgiveness continues to be withheld, the enemy will continue to harass and oppress, seeking to gain control of every part of the person's life.

Bitterness not only expresses itself internally in our feelings, but also in what we think.

What you think

Look at these words from Jeremiah:

> *'Wash your heart from evil, O Jerusalem,*
> *That you may be saved.*
> *How long will your **wicked** thoughts*
> *Lodge within you? ...*
> *"Your ways and your deeds*
> *Have brought these things to you.*
> *This is your evil. How bitter!*
> *How it has touched your heart!"*
> *My soul, my soul! I am in anguish! Oh, my heart!*
> *My heart is pounding in me;*
> *I cannot be silent,*
> *Because you have heard, O my soul,*
> *The sound of the trumpet,*
> *The alarm of war.'*   (Jeremiah 4:14, 18–19)

Despite denial, judgement and bitterness affect our thinking. They twist and distort our perception of life. As a result we start to form false assumptions about life. We develop thought patterns which form our beliefs. These affect our unconscious as well as our conscious mind. If we were told we were useless then, despite many achievements in our lives, we will still view ourselves as failures. We can be our own worst enemy sometimes, reinforcing the negatives. My wife Elaine's own testimony may help to illustrate this last point.

'From my early teens I can remember feeling "not good enough". Even though my family always approved of my achievements and encouraged me, I "knew" that as a person I was useless.

When I met Joff and married him, I could not believe that he could possibly love me ... I was ugly, useless and unlovable and didn't deserve loving. The first few years of our marriage were very difficult for Joff because I just couldn't receive his love. He showed me from the Bible that God loved me and that I had to love myself. I knew that God's Word was true and chose to believe it. Through many ups and downs and much perseverance I came to a place where I ruled my thinking and was able to receive Joff's love and God's.

Even so, underneath I "knew" I was still no good. I tried to be what I thought I should be and what everyone else thought I should be. But when tough issues arose or I failed in some way, I dropped back into my old way of thinking ... "Well you're useless anyway. What did you expect?"

God started to deal with me, showing me just how insecure I really was. Some of the emotions that started to surface were irritation (at the smallest things), anger, jealousy, intolerance, resentment and the fact that I had been trying to manipulate circumstances for years.

I knew I could not carry on with this conflict and asked some friends to pray for me. They prayed and broke a number of strongholds in my thinking. The next day I felt somewhat better, but knew God was bringing more garbage to the surface. Two days later, desperate to be set free, my friends prayed for me again. This time the Holy Spirit came on me powerfully and I began to shake, feeling a great pressure inside me wanting to break out. One friend had a picture of the story of the ugly duckling, and shared that

I was trying to be an ugly duckling, when really I was a swan.

Like a bolt of lightning, revelation came to me. I had wasted years trying to conform to an image of myself that God had not intended. Even other people had tried to squeeze me into "their" mould not mine. I laughed. I cried. I couldn't take it in. As people and experiences passed before my eyes, I could see it all. I was not a duck, I am a swan!

I prayed, forgiving and releasing the people who had tried to mould me into a duck. What release came to me that Monday evening! I realised that I had always been disappointed with myself, thinking I was an ugly duckling, when in fact all the time I was a swan. They cast out a religious spirit and broke the power of the wrong thinking.

After everyone had gone, I went upstairs, looked in the mirror and for the first time in my life, looked myself straight in the eye and said, "You're beautiful" and believed it!

What joy there now is in being me. I love myself and actually believe that other people love me and like me. It's fantastic! All the arguments have gone. The resentment, anger and jealousy have all gone. What a relief it is to stop trying to be something God never wanted me to be. I'm not an ugly duckling – I'm a swan!'

Elaine's experience is probably similar to hundreds of other people. Our distorted thinking influences everything. For example, if our father was a harsh, disciplinarian, we form the view that God, our heavenly Father is the same. We can also react in an equal and opposite way. If we were harshly disciplined as a child, we can make the decision that we will *never* do that with our children. When children eventually do come, we wonder why they are so insecure. Is the reason because we have set no limits for them? There are no consequences for their wrongdoing. Matters then become worse when you do decide to discipline them. This results in confusion. The child is left not knowing where they are with you. Their perception is that the goalposts keep moving. Instead of building security in the child, you reinforce insecurity ... fertile ground for the seed of offence and all we have touched on so far.

Chapter 9

The Fruit of Resentment

If those who have offended us have not been forgiven and released, then at some point the root of bitterness not only surfaces as a shoot, but grows into the fruit of resentment (see Figure 6).

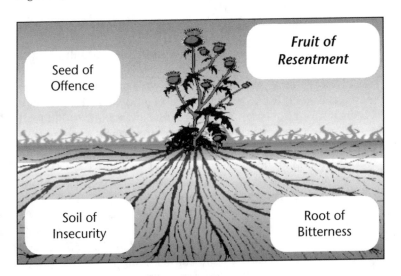

Figure 6

In 1992 Mount Etna on the island of Sicily was threatening to erupt. The pressure build-up was so great that lava burst out of the side of the volcano, flowing down the slopes and threatening to engulf a whole town. Drastic measures were needed to protect the town and its inhabitants.

Many people, even Christians, are like volcanoes waiting to erupt. The pain and heartache of their past bubbles away on the inside. Have you ever met 'prickly' people – quick-tempered, touchy people? They are the kind of people that you don't get too close to. They are similar to someone who has boils. Just dare to touch them! Anyone who has ever had a boil knows what I mean. If someone brushes past your boil, it is painful. Those people are usually like that because they are suppressing emotional pain inside themselves. Yet they try to put on a good face and say the right things. They were told as a child to 'Keep a stiff upper lip'; or 'Big boys don't cry'. All the emotion that needed to be expressed at the time just got buried.

The British 'stiff upper lip' is a con. It has deluded us into thinking we are in control. After all, what on earth would happen if all those emotions came out? If you have to live by the 'stiff upper lip'/'big boys don't cry' rules, you need to let God heal the hurts. He's the One who sent His Son to heal the brokenhearted. Psalm 34 says,

> *'The LORD is near to the brokenhearted*
> *And saves those who are crushed in spirit.'*   (Psalm 34:18)

The only way many know how to deal with pain and hurt from the past is to treat it like the basement of a house with rats. They lock the door to the basement, and throw away the key. But God does not want us to have a basement of unresolved issues within us. He wants to get the 'rats' out, so that He can cleanse and heal.

When Hezekiah became king, he set his heart to make a covenant with God. As part of his reforms, he gave instructions to the Levites concerning the temple.

> *'Then he said to them, "Listen to me, O Levites. Consecrate yourselves now, and consecrate the house of the LORD, the God of your fathers, and carry the uncleanness out from the holy place" ... So the priests went in to the inner part of the house of the LORD to cleanse it, and every unclean thing which they found in the temple of the LORD they brought out to the court of the house of the LORD. Then the Levites received it to carry out to the Kidron valley.'*   (2 Chronicles 29:5, 16)

It took fourteen men sixteen days to complete the cleansing. What followed can only be described as a revival. Sacrifices were made, worship began again, the Passover was celebrated and in

2 Chronicles 30:20 it says, *'So the Lord heard Hezekiah and healed the people.'* The people were so blessed they decided to celebrate the feast again for another seven days!

In 1 Corinthians Paul says,

> *'... do you not know that your body is a temple of the Holy Spirit who is in you, whom you have from God, and that you are not your own?'* (1 Corinthians 6:19)

God is far more interested in what we are like on the inside than what we are like on the outside. He is not too bothered whether we wear a flowery shirt or a plain shirt on a Sunday. Whether we wear jeans and a jumper or a three-piece suit doesn't really matter. What He is really interested in is our hearts. Jesus had harsh words for the teachers of the Law and the Pharisees who were more concerned about their external appearance than their relationship with God.

We, as individuals, are temples of God. Is there that which is 'unclean' in our inner part? No amount of excuses or denial makes the hurt go away. No amount of busyness ... even for God ... can deal with it. If there is that which is unclean, there is a need to go into the inner part and get the rubbish out. If the root of bitterness is not dealt with, it will produce the fruit of resentment in our lives. That resentment comes out in two ways.

What you say

My experience has convinced me that someone who is constantly talking negatively has a root of bitterness in their life. This has to be as a result of unforgiveness somewhere in their past.

> *'For the mouth speaks out of that which fills the heart.'* (Matthew 12:34)

This kind of person is a habitual fault finder! They find it so much easier to criticise others than find something good to say. Nothing ever seems to be right. The weather is never right. The government (whichever party is in power) is never right. Other drivers on the roads are wrong. In extremes it comes out in phrases like,

'Look at that idiot, his tie's not straight.'

'That guy next door really annoys me. Why does he have to have a ponytail?! He's not even fifty yet! And as for those tattoos ... they are *so* ungodly!'

'Why do people insist on filling their car windows with stickers of the places they've been?'

The issues don't really matter. In fact sometimes the more petty the issue is, the stronger they feel about it! If they do find something good to say, it usually has a hook:

'That was a reasonably pleasant meal darling, but couldn't you have made sure the cheesecake was totally defrosted before you served it?'

The fact that 'darling' may have slaved away in the kitchen for the last four hours has no relevance! Such negative statements quickly cross the line into judgement. The problem is that judgemental speech contaminates other people. In Hebrews 12:15 it says that when the root of bitterness springs up, it defiles many and causes trouble. Part of the reason the children of Israel failed to enter the promised land was because they grumbled and complained. A friend of mine once said that the Church could make a major impact on the world if Christians would stop grumbling and complaining like everyone else! Gossip is easy to listen to unless you train yourself not to. It's so easy to take on board negative talk about others. It is sad but true that Christians are not immune to this sin.

'Yes you are right. The elders have done it again; made decisions and not asked us what we think.'

'Well the elders in the last church I was in were the same. In fact they used to ...'

'I don't suppose we'll find a church where the elders are any different.'

'Birds of a feather flock together', so says the old proverb. Find one negative person and you are likely to find many of their friends are negative too. They tend to feed one another with their distorted thinking and perceptions.

What you do

Your behaviour and your lifestyle become negatively affected if you have a root of bitterness in your life. Such a root does not build up but tears down. It becomes difficult to relate to people.

People stay away from you because they don't want to get contaminated. Many aspects of life start to get affected.

Eating habits

Eating can be affected. 'Comfort eating' is an easy thing to slip into when there are still unresolved issues within. A dear lady I know used to eat a Mars bar every night in bed. Then God dealt with her about some hurts from the past. She forgave and released several people who had hurt her. The Mars bars stopped and she started to lose weight significantly. I also know a man whose ability to eat was a phenomenon! He was relatively slim and certainly not overweight. He did not have hollow legs, so what happened to the vast amounts of food he could tuck away? Nervous energy burnt it up. The tumult within was so great, it sapped him of energy. It was as much as he could do physically to satisfy his hunger. When energy is used up like that, creativity dwindles. The ability to think laterally gets submerged in the hurts that are mulled around on the inside. Much of this happens at an unconscious level.

Anorexia nervosa, the eating disorder, in my view comes from unresolved hurts deep within. The late Princess Diana made newspaper headlines with a speech to medical experts concerning her interest and insights into the causes of eating disorders, particularly among young people. She said, 'Many would like to believe that eating disorders are merely an expression of female vanity – not being able to get into a size 10 dress.' She dismissed this idea and said, 'From early childhood many had felt they were expected to be perfect but didn't feel they had the right to express their true feelings to those around them – feelings of guilt, of self revulsion and low personal esteem, creating in them a compulsion to "dissolve like a Disprin" and disappear.' She said that those who developed eating disorders found that by focusing their energies on controlling their bodies they had found a refuge from having to face painful issues at the centre of their lives. She also said that everyone could have a part to play in preventing such a thing to happen. 'As parents, teachers, family and friends, we have an obligation to care for our children, to encourage and guide, to nourish and nurture and to listen with love to their needs in ways which clearly show our children that we value them. They, in their turn, will then learn how to value themselves.'

I remember being moved to tears while watching the film *The Karen Carpenter Story* several years ago. The power of the Carpenters' lyrics, music and harmonies delighted millions. But a comment by one music paper reporter, calling Karen 'chubby', turned her against herself to the point that she determined to lose weight to become 'acceptable'. Her continual loss of weight damaged her heart and in 1983 she died of heart failure, aged 32. As a result the world was robbed of a great singer. The sadness in my heart was not just that she abused herself in the way she did. At one point in the film, the Carpenter family were with a psychiatrist treating Karen. He said that a common element in all patients suffering from *anorexia nervosa* was a particular fear. That fear was this: that if they didn't live up to family expectations they would not be loved. 'Are you saying that we don't love Karen?' asked her mother. 'No', came the reply, 'but have you told her that you love her?' The mother quickly replied, 'We don't do things that way, you show a person ... you don't tell them all the time.' Sadly that seemed to be the one thing Karen Carpenter needed.

Sleeping habits

Sleeping can be affected. When a person goes to bed they continually nurse and rehearse the hurt within. Sleep escapes them. They then become 'night owls' to ensure that when they go to bed, they are so tired that they have to sleep. In Ephesians it says,

> '*BE ANGRY, AND yet DO NOT SIN; do not let the sun go down on your anger, and do not give the devil an opportunity.*'
> (Ephesians 4:26–27)

My friend Victor Lorenzo says that when a person goes to bed angry they are sleeping with the enemy! Why? Although they may be asleep physically, their unconscious mind does not sleep. While asleep the unconscious mind will continue to process the things that have made us bitter and angry. This gives *'the devil an opportunity'*. When we wake, the offences don't seem more distant, they seem more intense. Victor says that every night before we sleep we should consciously forgive and release anyone who has hurt us that day. Then we can give our sleep to God where He can speak to us through dreams and visions.

Emotional and physical 'burn out' come from trying to keep all the plates spinning on the outside and yet on the inside, they are all crashing to the floor. As much as a person tries to rationalise the issues, they don't disappear. The results can be disastrous.

Physical effects

The physical effects can be numerous. The bitterness of the hurts within seep into a person's physical body. Ulcers, rheumatism, arthritis, gynaecological problems and cancer can all be caused by the root of bitterness.

I was out preaching in the street one day. I was making a point by saying that arthritis can be caused by bitterness, but that Jesus can heal people. An elderly lady in the crowd came forward waving her walking stick at me and shouting aggressively,

'I'm not a bitter person! I just hope you get arthritis one day. You don't know anything!'

Everyone else in the crowd could see that this lady's problem was that she was deeply bitter. The physical effects in her life were obvious: gnarled hands, stooped body, and venom on her tongue. Yet her thinking had become distorted by trying to cope with the pain within. The fruit of resentment was seen in her speech and her actions.

A friend of mine used to visit an eighty-six-year-old lady who was crippled with arthritis and rheumatism. One day he asked her about her childhood. She could remember the time her mother had brought her sister a beautiful dress for her birthday. She could also remember, with feeling, that her mother had not done so for her. She told my friend, 'I've hated my mother and sister ever since.' She died a bitter, twisted old lady a few months later, having held onto unforgiveness for eighty years.

I was speaking at a young couples' weekend a number of years ago and was asked to pray for a woman who had lost a baby over a year earlier. She had not been able to conceive since. She and her husband had been prayed for by the elders in their church, but nothing had changed. As we talked, it became apparent that she had become bitter towards both God and her husband.

We explained that, in our opinion, there is *never* any reason to need to forgive and release God! He never does anything wrong. He never hurts people despite the fact that we may perceieve circumstances in that way. He is intrinsically good. When we are hurt, both the hurts and the enemy twist our thinking to make us believe that God is not good.

She confessed that she had held resentment towards her husband. We asked her to forgive her husband there and then. She did so with tears. We then took her through a prayer of repentance for her bitterness towards God and her husband and prayed that God would again open her womb. A year later we heard that she was a mother again. Such is the power of forgiveness!

I am not saying all these physical problems are always caused by unforgiveness, but I am saying they can be. Bitterness seeks to affect every area of our lives.

Whenever I am asked to pray for the healing of someone with a similar condition, I usually start by asking if they have any unforgiveness in their heart. If the condition is a recent development, are there any issues recently that have provoked unforgiveness? If the condition is longstanding or persistent, is there unforgiveness going back to when the condition started?

A man was once asked by a friend if there was anything about him his wife did not like. After pausing for thought he said, 'Yes, there are just two things.' 'What are those?' his friend inquired. The man replied, 'Everything I say, and everything I do!'

The fruit of resentment is like that. It affects everything we say and everything we do.

Chapter 10

The Torture Chamber

'And his lord, moved with anger, handed him over to the torturers until he should repay all that was owed him. My heavenly Father will also do the same to you, if each of you does not forgive his brother from your heart.' (Matthew 18:34–35)

There are some Christians who always seem to be going on about the need for us to inherit 'the promises of God'. This is, of course, true. However, above is one promise that I rarely hear them wanting to inherit! Nevertheless it is a promise of Jesus. If you refuse to forgive, God the Father – and He is a loving heavenly Father at that – will hand you over to the torturers! We have already seen some of the natural consequences that we bring on ourselves through our bitterness, resentment and unforgiveness. Clearly if those natural consequences are not enough to persuade us to forgive, God has other means at His disposal.

What is the torture?

Under the old covenant there were dire consequences for the children of Israel who chose to walk in disobedience to the Lord. The covenant He made with them had conditions. There were blessings to inherit if they chose to obey but there were also curses if they disobeyed. You can read about them in Deuteronomy 28. Many of the curses were physical in nature, including different kinds of sickness, 'natural' disasters and oppression. There were others that were emotional, e.g. a trembling heart, despair of the soul, your life hanging in doubt before you, being in dread night and day, having no assurance of your life.

If the blessings were not enough motivation to obedience, then the curses certainly should have been! Let's face it, it would be difficult to come up with a more horrendous list of bad things that could happen to someone. A non-Jewish neighbour of a disobedient Israelite would look at what was happening to him and figure out that something was definitely wrong! Today, the life of someone who is full of resentment and bitterness, Christian or not, might be perceived by others as similar to the negative descriptions in Deuteronomy 28.

As Christians, however, we do not live under the constraints of the old covenant and are no longer under the Law or the curse of the Law. Praise God that under the new covenant:

> *'Christ redeemed us from the curse of the Law, having become a curse for us – for it is written, "CURSED IS EVERYONE WHO HANGS ON A TREE."'*   (Galatians 3:13)

There is no curse of the covenant for us who have put our faith in Jesus. But let's look again at 1 John 1:9:

> *'If we confess our sins, He is faithful and righteous to forgive us our sins and to cleanse us from all unrighteousness.'*

Remember that this was written to believers, not unbelievers. Cleansing from unrighteousness comes because of confession of sin. If we hold on to the sin of unforgiveness, neither confessing it nor repenting of it, then we will be unable to experience the healing and freedom Jesus won for us. Again let us remind ourselves of what Jesus taught:

> *'And forgive us our debts, as we also have forgiven our debtors ...*
> *For if you forgive others for their transgressions, your heavenly Father will also forgive you. But if you do not forgive others, then your Father will not forgive your transgressions.'*
>   (Matthew 6:12, 14–15)

So if you do not repent and confess your unforgiveness, there is no righteousness and no cleansing for you in that area of your life. The writer to the Hebrews says:

'See to it that no one comes short of the grace of God; that no root of bitterness springing up causes trouble, and by it many be defiled.' (Hebrews 12:15)

A root of bitterness coming from an angry, judgemental and unforgiving heart causes someone to 'come short of the grace of God'. The grace of God is defined as His unmerited, unearned or undeserved favour. To come short must mean that a measure of God's favour is withdrawn or held back from us. It cannot mean that we don't quite measure up to it or 'earn it' – as it is unmerited! That withdrawal may mean a lack of His protection from adverse circumstances or physical, mental and emotional health. That, of course, is not saying that bad things never happen to good people.

When there is evidence of anger and bitterness, it shouldn't be hard to make the connection. Even scientific research is making a connection between anger and the negative effects it has on health. In a report in the *Archives of Internal Medicine* in April 2002, a study of more than 1,000 men found that those who responded to stressful situations with feelings of anger were three times more likely to be diagnosed with heart disease before they turned 55. These men were five times as likely to have a heart attack before the age of 55. 'The findings suggest that learning to control anger might reduce the risk of premature heart disease, the leading cause of death in the US', Dr Patricia P. Chang, the study's lead author, said. Anger was also found to raise the risk of depression and anxiety.

We read earlier in 1 Corinthians 11 that some of the believers in Corinth were eating and drinking judgement on themselves (verse 29), that some were sick and some had even died as a result. A couple of verses later it says:

'But when we are judged, we are disciplined by the Lord so that we will not be condemned along with the world.' (1 Corinthians 11:32)

So the judgement of God in the here and now is His discipline, which as we read in chapter 7, is sorrowful. So we might say that the torture could be a mixture of:

- our own emotional and mental 'torture' as result of our judgemental attitudes and bitterness of heart

- the 'torture' of frustration as God removes His hand of blessing from us
- the 'torture' of the 'torturers' which we will look at next.

Who are the 'torturers'?

We saw in an earlier chapter that the devil can gain a foothold (literally, a place) in our lives if we are angry and do not forgive those who caused our anger (Ephesians 4:26–27). The use of the word 'devil' here does not mean that Satan himself will personally gain a place in you. 'Devil', here, is a generic term for Satan's evil minions – demons. We are used to hearing and using these kinds of figures of speech in modern language. Imagine a criminal saying to his accomplice, 'Look out! Here comes the law!'. He is actually referring to a police officer, not to the whole judiciary. 'The company has decided to give an extra day's holiday to the workforce this year', means the directors of the company have made the decision. The use of the word 'devil', therefore, must be determined by its context.

> *'Submit therefore to God. Resist the devil and he will flee from you.'*
> (James 4:7)

> *'Be of sober spirit, be on the alert. Your adversary, the devil, prowls about like a roaring lion, seeking someone to devour.'*
> (1 Peter 5:8)

The devil is not personally involved with every individual. God is omnipresent, the devil is not. In Britain, we do not expect Queen Elizabeth to stop her royal car and give a motorist parked on double yellow lines a parking ticket. That work is delegated, through an authority structure, to traffic police. So it is with the devil – anger, which is not resolved through forgiveness, gives the 'torturers' access to our lives to afflict, attack and oppress us.

However you look at the issue, it's all *bad news*! Although people suffer at the hands of the 'torturers', many never turn to God. They continue to do it 'My Way'. The curses mentioned above were to be released only on those who rejected God's way and chose to go their own way. Notice how many of the consequences of disobedience in Deuteronomy 28 affected the Israelites' health.

Today hospitals are filled with many people who are need-lessly sick. In a report in March 2002, Alcohol Concern told its annual conference that the cost to Britain's National Health Service is as high as £3 billion a year. Over 28,000 people are admitted to hospital every year in England and Wales because they are dependent on alcohol or have been poisoned by it. In another study a couple of years earlier at the Royal Bolton Hospital, a fifth of all psychiatric admissions over six months were alcohol related. It is estimated that 20% of patients that go to see their GP are likely to be excessive drinkers. Why do people turn to alcohol? To numb the pain within. To help them cope with the disappointments and hurts that have come their way.

For others, the only answers for recurring sickness is treatment by drugs. The real cause is often undiscovered. Friends of mine who are doctors tell me they see a continual stream of people whose health could change for the better if they were willing to forgive and release those who have hurt them. One doctor reckoned that up to 70% of his patients were there as a result of unforgiveness.

A psychiatrist friend of mine often feels powerless with her patients. The reason is that the answer to many people's emo-tional and mental needs is not prescribed on the National Health Service.

Many people today are turning to alternative medicine. Why? Mainstream medicine does not seem to come up with the goods for them and the fear of unknown side-effects adds to their suspicion. Another major reason that practitioners of alternative remedies are getting more clients is that they have 'time' for their clients. They will actually listen to them and try to understand the underlying issues. Unfortunately many people are still going to be sick even though they have had their feet rubbed, muscles tested, backs manipulated, bath water smelling nice, legs crossed and mind emptied. Why? Because they remain in the 'Torture Chamber of Unforgiveness'.

Chapter 11

Opening the Books

A stubborn heart

Some people make excuses for their lack of forgiveness.

'I could never forgive them for what they've done to me. It hurts too much.'

'I tried to once, but it didn't seem to make any difference.'

'Anyway, it's their fault ... They are the ones that have done wrong. They should be coming to me.'

These are all the excuses of a stubborn heart. Saying 'I could never forgive' is being stubborn. It's opening the door to the torture chamber and closing the door on God and His forgiveness.

Do we sometimes wonder why we are frequently falling into sin, constantly falling prey to temptation? Is it because in our hearts there is no righteousness, there is no cleansing, there is no forgiveness, because we have not forgiven others? I have come across a number of Christians who deal with the hurts by saying, 'Well, I've tried to forgive six times already, but it keeps coming back. So I just keep on forgiving them every time I think about it. Like Jesus said: seventy times seven.'

But this is not what the parable in Matthew 18 teaches. The parable teaches that you forgive the person and release them from the debt. When the account is settled, that is the end of the matter. The king did not have to forgive the servant again and again. Why not? Because the account had been settled once and for all. God does not have a 'record card' of all the wrong things we have done ... unless we are deliberately living in unforgiveness. We have a clean sheet. That is how He wants our relationship with Him to be. The point of the parable is that accounts were settled and closed.

God wants to set His people free! Most people, if not all, have been brokenhearted at some point in their lives. That is why part of the commission of Jesus was to bind the broken hearts and set the captives free. Many people are captive to their emotions. They are frightened of letting them be exposed for fear of what might come out. But Jesus wants to set us free in every way.

'So if the Son sets you free, you will be free indeed.'
(John 8:36 NIV)

'It was for freedom that Christ set us free; therefore keep standing firm and do not be subject again to a yoke of slavery.'
(Galatians 5:1)

The debtors

Here is a list of the people who are the most likely to have hurt us and caused us to feel owed: father, mother, brother, sister, child, auntie, uncle, grandfather grandmother, friend, teacher, husband, wife, and if you are a Christian, church leaders.

In other words, all the people who tend to be close to us. The ones who should bring most security are often the ones who have the power to hurt us the most. Many of the hurts they have inflicted on us may have been unintentional, *yet they are real to us*. If they have not been dealt with, they can be as painful today as they were the day they happened.

The wife of a husband that has had an affair has been robbed. First, her husband has taken the love and affection that should have been given to his wife and given it to someone else. Secondly, the lover has robbed the wife of her husband. Both need forgiving and releasing.

The debts

Although parables are not allegories in the strict sense, there is much that can be understood of forgiveness if we look more closely at Matthew 18.

When the man who owed the king ten thousand talents came before him, the money the king was owed may have been made up of various items. Four hundred barrels of oil, two hundred sacks of wheat, twenty donkeys, etc. The king would have had an account book showing the entries, or copies of the invoices, complete with dates and the details of each transaction. Clearly the slave had not paid anything to the king at the time the king wished to settle accounts. So it is within us. We keep records of the wrongs done against us, noting the who, when, where and how in our memory and emotions. As much as we try to bury the issues, rationalise them or just deny them, God has ways of calling us to account. My prayer is that the Holy Spirit will bring you illumination of any debts outstanding that have not been dealt with.

The accuser

The brain is an amazing organ. It has the capacity to not only recall memory but also to recall the emotions that went with the memory. That is why nostalgia is big business! If we hear a song from the time we were pursuing a handsome young man or a beautiful young lady, we don't just remember the words. We can remember the romantic feelings that we had at that time. We may well be able to feel our heart start to beat faster!

This is true from a positive perspective, and it is also true negatively. When the enemy comes to help us rehearse the hurts, he is never general. He doesn't say, 'Well you just had a bad childhood.' The enemy of our souls can be as accurate as the laser-guided bombs we saw used in the Gulf wars. He will take the 'videotape' of our memory and spin it back to specific incidents. He will say, 'Do you remember the time when your friend broke your bike? He didn't even offer to pay or mend it. He just laughed. So did Frank and John who were with him.'

The truth is this. Although we may be owed literally, inside we feel owed more because the laughter of those boys humiliated us. They robbed us of self-esteem. They made us feel powerless and pathetic. Inside, that can still hurt.

'Do you remember when the headmaster told you that you would never pass any exams because "You're a waste of space"'? Those words can have seemed like a curse that hung over us for the rest of our educational life. When we failed our exams, we came to the conclusion that maybe the headmaster was right. We then started to believe him. 'I'm no good. I'm a failure. I'll never be good at anything.' The Accuser was always quick to agree.

Can you remember when your father or mother spoke, out of frustration to you, words that wounded you deep down on the inside? You can think about them right now and still feel how you felt then. You can feel the knot in your stomach, the tightness in your throat, the tear in your eye. At these times it is no good claiming, 'It's all dealt with'. Your emotions know that these things are not resolved.

The bully

At secondary school, a boy who was in my year had set about another boy with a belt and beaten him quite badly. The deputy head teacher came to our class to ask if anyone knew who had done it. The boy who had been attacked was too frightened to 'split'. I put my hand up amidst gasps from my form mates. They knew the consequences that I would face from the bully. Several days later, on the school playing field, I was told, 'Eddy wants to see you.' I anxiously went across to see him. He put his face right up to my face.

'Wait till the end of term, Day. I'm going to get you!'

With that, he head butted me, sending me reeling to the floor. His mates jeered. My mates were surprised I got off so lightly. I lived in fear for the next four weeks, unsure of what my fate would be at his hands.

I told nobody how scared I was. I bought a book on Judo and practised in my bedroom! I tried to convince myself I could beat him in a fair fight. The problem was, he didn't fight fair.

The last day of term came. I hadn't seen him all day, but knew he had been up to no good. I had done some serious praying that day even though I wasn't really walking with God at that time. I had my plan hatched. If he was there with his mates I would run. If he was there by himself I would fight. My heart was in my mouth as I walked to the school gates.

He never showed up at all. He was too busy letting down tyres in the school bike sheds.

I saw him again nearly ten years later, on a visit to my home town. He obviously didn't recognise me, but a chill went up my spine, and a knot came into my stomach when I saw him. Sometime later I heard that in a domestic dispute while he was drunk, he climbed over the balcony edge of his fifth floor flat, fell off and died. When I heard that, I was glad. I remember saying to

my brother, 'He finally got what he deserved.' I thought the issue
was closed. Then God started to speak to me.

Mercy – the key factor

Grace, I was once told, is getting what we don't deserve; whereas
mercy is not getting what we do deserve.

'Are you going to forgive him?' came the familiar voice into
my spirit.

'But he's dead now, Lord.'

'You were robbed by him on that school field and you know
it,' came the reply.

I never had forgiven him. I had carried judgement in my heart
towards him ever since the incident on the school playing field. I
thought it was just one of those experiences you went through. It
toughens you up for the real world and helps to shape your
character. I now thought back to those fourth-form days. I not
only felt angry at what he had done to me, but angry for the
others he had hurt. I felt in my heart again the sense of injustice
at how he had treated me and made me look weak and foolish. I
also felt that he had robbed me of security. I had never known
whether he would be waiting on the corner of my road when I
got home from school.

Even though he was dead and buried, I knew I had unforgiveness in my heart towards him. That boy could never pay me back
what he took from me. I forgave him specifically for the things
he had done wrong to me. I also released him from what I felt he
owed me in terms of self-esteem and security. I asked God for
forgiveness for my unforgiveness and the bitterness in my heart.

Did he deserve it? No. I felt he deserved to have done to him
what he had done to others. But neither did I deserve the
forgiveness God gave me. God had mercy on me. He didn't give
me what I really deserved. It was because God had mercy on me,
forgiving and releasing me, that I was able to do the same.
Releasing forgiveness to a dead man did not change him. But it
changed me. I saw afresh the mercy of God.

It was Shylock in Shakespeare's *Merchant of Venice* that wanted
his pound of flesh. We can be the same. We want what we are
due. If we don't get it, we feel owed. We would like to get our
own back on those who have taken from us and not given in
return. Choosing not to get our own back, but forgiving instead,

is having mercy. The whole point of the parable is that the king had mercy. He did not give that slave what he deserved.

Who's to blame?

There are some hurts people take on board because of their own bad attitudes. I remember hearing of a person who was praying through some issues of forgiveness, and saying, 'I want to forgive my sister for being better at school than me.' Fortunately, those who were praying with the person stopped them. There was no need to forgive her sister. There was a need to repent of jealousy.

We must not put the blame for our bad attitudes onto other people. We must take responsibility for our own sin and our own sinful attitudes. We must take responsibility for our own jealousy, our own selfishness, our own pride, and repent and seek God's forgiveness. Neither should we excuse ourselves by blaming it on demons!

There are also times when we are genuinely hurt by people who did not understand what they were doing. How many times when something has happened have we heard the words, 'Don't blame them, they didn't do it deliberately'. Yet inside we felt that they were responsible for what happened. It is quite possible for people to hurt us, and sin against us, unknowingly. Many hurts we have experienced, particularly from loving parents, may have come in this way. If we were to think about ourselves, we would probably find we have done the same. Do we not want the people who we unintentionally hurt to forgive us? When Jesus was on the cross, he said,

> *'Father, forgive them; for they do not know what they are doing.'*
> (Luke 23:34)

If Jesus found it necessary to forgive those who did not understand what they were doing, how much more should we?

Chapter 12

Settling Accounts

How do you do it?

This is the part in the book where the 'we' becomes 'you'!

Prepare to do business with God

Ask the Holy Spirit to open up areas where your emotions have been damaged; where you feel *owed*; where you've been *hurt*. Maybe you can feel an ache in your heart right now. In your mind you could be saying, 'If only things could have been different; if only that didn't happen.' Hope deferred has made your heart sick. You need to ask God to allow you to become 'connected' to the hurt and the pain in your heart. This is really important if you are to know God's healing on the inside. In fact, it is probably the only way you will actually be able to forgive *from the heart*.

If this becomes just an intellectual exercise, you may 'forgive' at a mental level, but leave your emotions unchanged. Your mind may have the satisfaction of knowing you have 'done the right thing', but the pain in your heart will remain and not get healed.

You may be the kind of person who 'rules' everything. When you pray, you can be honest with the Lord in about any way in which you have 'excused' the injustices you have suffered. You can admit that you have suppressed or denied your feelings. This can be fairly difficult. Having someone else to help you pray to break down these defence mechanisms (strongholds) can be invaluable. If you have been proud of your ability to handle situations in this way, you will need to repent of your pride too!

Why do some people find they are still hurting when they think about a person who they thought they had forgiven. There can be a number of reasons. Usually, it is because they mentally 'forgave' but it never touched their heart. Sometimes there are other issues with the person that need forgiving. Occasionally the mind has chosen to 'block out' painful memories, and as a result forgiveness is not released into those areas. This is often true in cases of childhood trauma, e.g. sexual abuse. The other reason is that pain is still felt after forgiveness has taken place is because of the grief associated with the 'loss'. I will talk about this in chapter 15.

The answer is to ask the Holy Spirit to reveal any unresolved issues. This is not 'navel' inspecting, it's account clearing!

Make an invoice

Get a piece of paper and write down a list of the people who have hurt you and what they did to hurt you. Don't rationalise ... 'It wasn't really my dad's fault ...' if inside you feel it was. Be specific not general. For example:

- *not*:

    Dad – for being a pain in the neck;

- *but*:

    Dad – for not encouraging me when I did well at school.
    – for constantly going on about my ears in front of others.
    – for never telling me he loved me.
    – for telling my friend I wet the bed.
    – etc.

Making an invoice can be the first time we really come to terms with the amount of hurt within and admit the fact that we are owed by others.

Count the cost of releasing them

Realise that they can never pay you back what you feel owed. The king knew that the servant was *unable* to pay, not just *unwilling*. In the same way, we can never 'pay back' what we owe to God. We could go to church every Sunday (and Wednesday); have a quiet time every morning; take communion every day and give money to the poor. We could even go to the mission field; but we can never pay Him back.

It may be helpful at this point to think about how much God has forgiven you. When you became a Christian, you possibly said a 'prayer for salvation'. This probably included what I call 'blanket' words of repentance and forgiveness. In other words, we repent of everything generally and ask for forgiveness of everything generally. Although our hearts may be genuine and we get born again, we miss the greatness of the grace of God. If we had a true understanding of what it cost God to forgive us for each specific sin we have committed, the cost of forgiving others would seem insignificant by comparison.

Counting the cost also means no longer having an emotional weapon against the person who has hurt us. When we have forgiven, released and received inner healing, we once again become vulnerable.

Have mercy on them

As you pray, admit your emotions to God. It may be that you will need to express the anger you have felt towards the person you are going to forgive. I can remember being let down very badly by a colleague who was also a good friend. It was not possible to express my anger to him personally as he had become very ill. Expressing my anger to him would not have helped his recovery. So I found a place where I could not be heard and stomped round the room letting the walls take the full force of my anger! And yes, occasionally I shouted. I used expressions like: 'You have made me so angry because you have not . . . ' and 'You have made me so angry because you have . . . '

I probably spent an hour doing this! Then, when I knew I had fully expressed my anger, I started the process of forgiving him. In one sense, I was showing mercy to him by venting my anger at the walls! If you have felt that those who have hurt you deserve the same thing to happen to them, be honest as you pray and tell the Lord. If they crashed your car you may feel, or have felt, that they deserve to have their car crashed. If they made fun of you and put you down in front of others, you may feel that is what should happen to them. You may feel that they need to be made to feel how they made you feel. You may feel they actually deserve worse in return. Determine that even if you had the person in front of you now, and had the power to do anything to them, that you would show them mercy.

Forgive and release them for each and every incident

I have prayed through forgiveness with many people and heard them say, 'Lord I forgive my dad for not showing me love, and for not encouraging me when I needed it.' They then go on to someone else, but I stop them. I explain that it is good and right to forgive him, but that there is a big hole in their heart where they never had that love, because they never heard the words,

'Son I love you. Son I think you're tremendous. Son you really ride your bike well. Son I really appreciate you for just being you. There's nobody else like you in the whole world.'

There is a debt outstanding where those words which *should* have been spoken, were not. Why? Because fathers *should* say those things, even as the heavenly Father spoke to His Son. As a result, people need not only to *forgive* their fathers for the fact that they did what they did, but they also need to *release* their fathers from the debt as well.

The king in Matthew 18 did not just forgive the man for not paying him the ten thousand talents he owed. He actually released him from the debt as well.

For many people, praying through these kinds of issues can be pretty traumatic and emotional. I am convinced that it is better to have one or two Christian friends with you if you are going to pray through emotionally hurtful issues. They can encourage and help you to see things clearly. They can pray for you and help you to pray appropriately. They will also be witnesses to the fact that you have forgiven and released.

When you pray, speak out loud words like these: 'Father, in Jesus' name, I forgive [the person's name] for [the offence or list of offences] and for the effect it has had on my life, and right now I release them from what they owe me.' Words have power. Proverbs 18:21 says:

> 'Death and life are in the power of the tongue.'
> (Proverbs 18:21)

As you are praying out these things, you are speaking powerful words that will break the power of the enemy's chains in your life. You will also break the power of control that your unfor-giveness has held you under. All the time you did not forgive, you were in effect allowing the person and their offence to control you in your thoughts and emotions. When you forgive a dead person, you break the power of control from beyond the grave!

Cross out each item on your 'invoice' as you forgive and release the person. Remember, if you pray, 'Lord this is the fifteenth time I've had to forgive them', then you did not forgive them the other fourteen times! The accounts are still open. If you keep score, you have not forgiven.

Then ask God to forgive them and bless them. That kind of praying is powerful. It is also the test as to whether you have actually forgiven and released them.

> *'But I say to you who hear, love your enemies, do good to those who hate you, bless those who curse you, pray for those who mistreat you.'*   (Luke 6:27–28)

I have found tremendous personal release, having forgiven those who have mistreated me, by praying God's blessing over them. The enemy definitely does not like it!

Ask God to forgive you for your unforgiveness

While you had unforgiveness in your heart, there was no right-eousness and no cleansing in that area. He can now forgive you on the basis of what Jesus said:

> *'For if you forgive men when they sin against you, your heavenly Father will also forgive you.'*   (Matthew 6:14 NIV)

Get the person(s) with you to pray healing into your life

> *'Therefore, confess your sins to one another, and pray for one another so that you may be healed. The effective prayer of a righteous man can accomplish much.'*   (James 5:16)

I cannot emphasise this scriptural injunction enough. Some people never get free from issues of unforgiveness because they have never confessed them to anyone else. They have kept it inside them. This is why it is good to have others with you to hear your confession.

Where you have been wounded emotionally, there will be a need for healing. Just admitting you have been hurt does not bring healing. It just takes the sticking plaster off the wound. The person who is with you can lay hands on you and pray for you for this. It may be appropriate to pray for you after you have finished forgiving each person or each issue. As there may be a lot of emotion involved, this should not be rushed.

Joel 2:25 says that God can restore (or make up) the years that the locusts have eaten. The locusts were a destructive army that the Lord was to release against His people because of their disobedience. The promise of God's Spirit being poured out on all flesh at the end of Joel 2 follows the call to repentance, and the promise of restoration.

God can restore the areas of your life where the enemy has eaten away at you emotionally and robbed you of righteousness, peace and joy. Those who are with you should pray this restoration, asking the Holy Spirit to come and refresh you and fill you.

We have found that a person may need several hours to talk through the issues and pray. Sometimes, several sessions are needed so this could take weeks or even months. Those who are praying with and for another person need love, compassion and sensitivity. They must also be prepared to confront the person they are praying with if there is evidence that they are withholding forgiveness or repentance. Healing is usually a process, but time is not the healer, God is. Jesus came to bind the broken hearts and to heal them.

Tear up the invoice

The account is now settled and closed. If the enemy ever comes back to you and says, 'Do you remember what that person did to you?' don't talk back to him. Turn your response into a prayer of thanksgiving. You can say, 'Yes, Lord. I remember the day when I wrote that down as a debt, and I forgave that person and I released them. They don't owe me a thing any more. Not only that, You have forgiven all my debts. You've had mercy on me. You've released me. Hallelujah!'

The accuser will disappear quickly! Rejoice in God's goodness. Set your will to forgive and release any others that God shows you.

Chapter 13

Staying Free

All that we have looked at so far, I have called forgiving and releasing. But really, it is only *biblical* forgiveness. To forgive someone is to release them from the debt they owe. It is what the 'gospel' is all about. The Good News is that God has forgiven us because of Jesus. Our response is to forgive those who have sinned against us. That is the practical implication.

It is tragic that many Christians believe that, but do not practice it. A person who says, 'Praise God I'm going to heaven now. I just hope that I don't have to spend eternity with *that* creep,' has not understood what Jesus had to say about forgiveness!

The whole concept of forgiveness in the Bible is to do with debts and debtors; having mercy on those who cannot pay back what they owe. Sadly, much Christian teaching on forgiveness has missed the vital aspect of *releasing* others as well as forgiving. That is one reason for writing this book. Another reason is so that new Christians can be given something to help them avoid the mistake made by the unforgiving servant.

A number of churches I know devote a whole session of their 'new beginnings' course for new Christians to forgiving and releasing. At an early stage these new believers get to clear out years of garbage which the enemy has dumped on them. These Christians have found that it sets a foundation of forgiveness in their spiritual lives which enables them to make good progress in their walk with God. Of course, this does not make them perfect overnight!

I love training people, who have worked through their issues, how to minister this to others. They are keen. They know what a dynamic effect it has had in their own lives (the final chapter of this book includes some of their stories).

Sometimes, in ministering to people, the strongholds of unforgiveness seem to find physical expression under the power of the Holy Spirit's presence. This may include pains in the stomach, the sense of being strangled (particularly when it actually comes to speaking the words of forgiveness), burping and belching, yawning, shaking, falling over, crawling around the floor, as well as weeping and loud cries of anguish. These strongholds can be broken through prayer.

In this 'clean up' process, we sometimes come across demons. Some manifestations mentioned above may be a sign of demonic activity, but discernment and sensitivity to the Holy Spirit is needed. Sometimes the demons reveal their work as anger, hatred, rejection, jealousy, pride, and similar negative characteristics. They are confronted and cast out. It is beyond the scope of this book to explain the casting out of demons. Sometimes the very act of forgiveness brings instant deliverance.

People who have been 'chronic seekers' of the baptism of the Holy Spirit have often found it was unforgiveness that was the blockage. Those who have sought the Lord for physical healing and found none sometimes find that there is unresolved unforgiveness in their past that they were not consciously aware of. The releasing of forgiveness to others and the receiving of forgiveness themselves is often the key to their healing.

How to stay free

Set your will to forgive and release anyone who has hurt or offended you (in the past or present)

Not only that, you must make a quality decision of the will to forgive anyone that hurts or offends you in the future, however great or small the offence.

At one time, major changes were about to take place in my life. I knew that I was going to face a time of conflict and confrontation with people I both loved and respected. While praying one day, I felt the Lord say to me, 'Even if they drive a ten ton truck over you, you must let them. You must not fight them; they are your brothers. You must only pray for them and bless them. I will use the circumstances to shape your character, and develop greater faith in Me.' The following months were some of the most difficult of my whole life.

I had to encounter accusation both openly and behind my

back. I had to face criticism, some of which was justified, and some of which was unjustified. Many things that were said wounded me deeply. I was not alone in this. My wife, too, had her fair share of 'going through the mill'. But in it all, we were determined to do what God had said: forgive, release and bless those who hurt us. At one particular confrontation, I was told all the things I had not done and all the things I never would do. This left me feeling that the ten ton truck had been driven over my emotions, stopped, reversed back over me, put into forward gear and driven over me again! I remember sliding under the door that I had walked through 30 minutes earlier!

I had an underlying belief that these people were actually for me. It just did not feel like it at the time! I also had a few friends who really knew what I was going through. They helped me to sort out the wheat from the chaff and encouraged me to continue to forgive and to bless. They were also able to pray for me and minister healing to me as I have described previously. God really did use the whole episode to strengthen my faith and my emotions. It again confirmed to me personally the real power of forgiveness.

Forgiveness is spiritual warfare and will weaken the enemy's ability to attack you and gain a place in your heart. Determine right now, before the Lord, that you too, are going to set your will to forgive and release others.

Get to work on the soil of insecurity in your heart

A gardener will rake over his soil to remove any lumps of stone or debris that would stop his plants from having a firm foundation for their roots. He will also dig in manure to enrich the soil. Find the areas in your life where you are insecure. Most of us are a mixture of security and insecurity in differing degrees. We may feel secure in one setting but not in another. If you are not sure where you are insecure, ask your best friend! All soil is susceptible to weeds. There is a story of a young minister who went to visit an old man. As he walked up the path to the cottage door, he admired the superb garden. It was beautifully laid out and well stocked with flowers. His opening gambit was to say, 'I see that the Lord has given you a beautiful garden.' 'Yes,' came the quick reply, 'but you should have seen it when it was left to Him!'

If we do not attend to the garden of our heart, it is easy for the weeds to grow. They will choke the good seed that God wants to put in. We must diligently nurture the soil so that the good seed can produce a bumper crop of righteousness.

Root out unbelief from your heart

This must start by laying the axe to the root of any thinking pattern you have adopted that is contrary to the Word of God. Second Corinthians 10:4–5 talks about fortresses or strongholds of the mind. These lofty things are raised up against the knowledge of God. They can be destroyed by the weapons of our warfare: prayer and the Word of God.

Romans 10:17 says that faith comes by hearing. Although the context here is to do with faith for salvation, the principle holds true in other areas. The verb 'hearing' is in the present-continuous tense. This allows us to interpret the text by saying, faith comes by hearing and hearing and hearing (i.e. by continually hearing).

If you have been constantly told that you are useless, you can end up believing it is true, putting your faith in the fact of it being true, and finally living as if it is true. But that thinking and that believing are directly contrary to the Word of God! We must 'feed' the soil of our hearts with the Word of God. It is true that God has chosen the foolish, weak, base and despised things of the world (1 Corinthians 1:27–28) but what does verse 30 say?

> *'It is because of him that you are in Christ Jesus, who has become for us wisdom from God – that is, our righteousness, holiness and redemption. Therefore, as it is written: "Let him who boasts boast in the Lord."'* (1 Corinthians 1:30–31 NIV)

Develop your personal relationship with the 'Gardener'

Many books have been written on this subject. The key is understanding the difference between knowing about God and knowing God. Some people could tell you enough details about the British royal family that you would think they knew the Queen personally. In reality they may have never met or spoken to any of them. Many Christians know lots of detail about God, but don't really know Him personally.

Sung worship, Bible reading, prayer and fellowship with other believers are important and helpful to our Christian growth. But don't be deceived into thinking those activities *are* our relationship with God. Sometimes they can be a substitute for the real thing. Knowing God is not to do with technique, it has to do with time. The way you really get to know Him is by spending time with Him. That time may not necessarily mean doing any of the above activities. Communicate with the Lord constantly, whether you are walking down the street, driving the car, hanging out the washing or taking a bath. You can be conscious of His felt presence with you on a daily and hourly basis. If you have a daily 'devotional' time, it should be the cream on the cake of your relationship with the Lord, not the cake itself. The best times of intimacy in a marriage come as a result of good communication throughout the hours and days preceding.

Sow the good seed of the Word of God into your prepared soil

We are now 'in Christ'. Find the book of Ephesians and highlight or underline all the verses that tell us who or what we are 'in Christ' or 'in Him'. Find the verses that tell you what He is in us. Turn these scriptures over in your mind again and again and again. It will be like turning 'spiritual fertiliser' into the soil of your heart.

If you have been fed worry, anxiety and fear all your life, take time to read Matthew 6:25–34. Three times Jesus tells us *'Do not be anxious.'* There are wonderful promises here that Jesus has made to all those who are prepared to put His kingdom first their lives.

Matthew 5:23–26 gives Jesus' way of reconciling two Christians. If you realise there is an issue between you and another Christian, go and sort it out straight away. But remember that there are ways of handling conflict that can cause hurt. I remember someone coming up to me at the end of a meeting where I had just preached:

'Joff, I just want you to know that I have really forgiven you for what you did to me.'

I couldn't even think of having spoken to the man for several weeks. 'Oh what was that?' I asked.

'You didn't smile back at me when I smiled at you last Sunday. I felt really hurt, but I forgave you this morning,' came the response.

I replied as best I could, 'Well I think you could have got that sorted out between you and the Lord.' I didn't have time to talk to him about his insecurity, bad attitudes and other hang ups. He went off feeling fine. I went off feeling that I needed to forgive him for being so stupid! Most church leaders will identify with this story!

It is not always necessary to confront the person who has hurt you. This is especially true if they *do not know* they have hurt you. In fact confronting them may only cause more hurt and bad feeling. But there are times where we must leave our 'offering' and go to see the person with whom we have an issue. I believe this kind of forgiving lifestyle is the essence of authentic Christianity.

Chapter 14

Forgiveness Brings Healing

Healing for the individual

This healing starts with the restoration of our broken relationship with God through repentance and faith (see appendix A). We have also seen that having been forgiven by God, we must then forgive and release others. As we do this we are released from the 'torturers' who may have brought assorted problems into our lives. Healing, whether emotional or physical, can then be effected in our lives by the power of the Holy Spirit.

Healing for the family

Most family rifts continue because the members are unwilling to forgive and release those who have hurt them. The resulting feuds can continue for generations. Each succeeding generation is fed with anger towards and hatred for the other side. Things need not continue in this way, or even start.

Parents must teach their children the principles of forgiveness from an early age. We sought to help our children do this in two ways. Firstly, if Elaine and I caused hurt to each other when our children were around, we didn't just 'make up' at bedtime. The children got to hear us ask for and receive forgiveness from one another. This can be very humbling! Secondly, as a result of seeing Dad eating humble pie and apologising, they were taught *why* it is important for us to do this.

As a result our children have discovered how to release forgiveness to each other when they are wronged. They have also learned how to say sorry and ask for forgiveness when they have wronged someone else. This has helped to create an environment in our home where there are no 'undercurrents' of bitterness. At school and college they are also able to put into practice what they have learned at home. With the inevitable hassle of relating to peers there is plenty of opportunity for forgiving and releasing! This has not made them weak or soft though. Their ability to handle conflicts while young has built solid character into their lives.

As parents, therefore, we must not only teach, but model forgiveness for our children.

Healing for the local church

Every church, at one time or another, has hassle between its members. This is because the church is made up of imperfect people! In some churches, unresolved issues have caused division and led to the church splitting. This often results in much heart-ache and bitterness. Sometimes the resulting church factions may fail to grow significantly because of their unforgiveness towards each other. Many such conflicts could be resolved if churches and individual Christians would obey the Bible. Jesus gave some clear instructions about handling conflict.

> 'You have heard that the ancients were told, "YOU SHALL NOT COMMIT MURDER" and "Whoever commits murder shall be liable to the court."
>
> But I say to you that everyone who is angry with his brother shall be guilty before the court; and whoever says to his brother, "You good-for-nothing," shall be guilty before the supreme court; and whoever says, "You fool," shall be guilty enough to go into the fiery hell.
>
> Therefore if you are presenting your offering at the altar, and there remember that your brother has something against you, leave your offering there before the altar, and go; first be reconciled to your brother, and then come and present your offering.
>
> Make friends quickly with your opponent at law while you are with him on the way, so that your opponent may not hand you over to the judge, and the judge to the officer, and you be thrown into prison. Truly I say to you, you will not come out of there until you have paid up the last cent.' (Matthew 5:21–26)

The implication in these verses is that a brother has something against you because of something you have said or done. If you are suddenly reminded of this fact, Jesus said that it is your responsibility to go and put things right – even if it means missing the start of the Sunday meeting, Wednesday evening Bible study, or a round on the golf course!

Once more we see Him referring to the *prison* and, by implication, the *prison officer* (as in the jailer of Matthew 18:34–35), as well as to the issue of not *paying up*. These are all phrases we are familiar with. It seems that if you know someone is holding unforgiveness towards you, and you are not prepared to get it sorted out, God will deal with you as well as with them. They may have been delivered over to the jailers because of their unforgiveness towards you. However, if you do not get the situation resolved, you could be heading for the jail as well!

Sometimes relationships get broken because of:

- a careless attitude
- a misunderstanding
- non communication
- sin

but, it is still *your* responsibility to get the issue resolved.

Before the parable of the unforgiving servant in Matthew 18, Jesus gives similar instructions to the ones above.

> *'If your brother sins, go and show him his fault in private; if he listens to you, you have won your brother.*
>
> *But if he does not listen to you, take one or two more with you, so that* BY THE MOUTH OF TWO OR THREE WITNESSES EVERY FACT MAY BE CONFIRMED.
>
> *If he refuses to listen to them, tell it to the church; and if he refuses to listen even to the church, let him be to you as a Gentile and a tax collector.*
>
> *Truly I say to you, whatever you bind on earth shall have been bound in heaven; and whatever you loose on earth shall have been loosed in heaven.'*   (Matthew 18:15–18)

If you become aware that your brother has sinned, what is your responsibility? It is not to go the church leaders and tell them; not at this stage anyway. Go to the person in private. Often our own hang-ups and fear of rejection will try to prevent us doing this, but do it we must.

Jesus then says what to do if you are not received by the person. Only after that step does the issue become one for the church leadership. Notice too that what Jesus said regarding binding and loosing was to do with forgiveness. Although it may also refer to church discipline, He was saying that if you refuse to release forgiveness here, it will not be released in heaven. But if you forgive and release here on earth, it will be forgiven and released in heaven. This is how we can understand what Jesus said:

> '*But if you do not forgive men their sins, your Father will not forgive your sins.*' (Matthew 6:15 NIV)

Healing for the body of Christ

It is estimated that there are some 25,000 denominations across the world, and the number is growing. This does rather seem to contradict the prayer of Jesus in John 17.

> '*I do not ask on behalf of these alone, but for those also who believe in Me through their word; **that they may all be one;** even as You, Father, are in Me and I in You, that they also may be in Us, so that the world may believe that You sent Me.*'
> (John 17:20–21)

Twenty-five thousand does not equal one! However, there can be diversity as well as unity. Sadly, many Christians in one denomination look at those in another with fear and suspicion. For some the fear is real because they have been hurt by some of those others.

Again, the answer is the same. Those that have caused hurt must be forgiven and released. This must take place first with church leaders. They themselves must forgive and release those who have hurt and wounded them, if they are to bring their churches into freedom. This will not resolve the many theological and doctrinal differences that separate the groups. However, it will pave the way for relational reconciliation. Forgiveness and reconciliation are the very heart of Christianity.

Healing for the world

The 'United' Nations are constantly looking for ways to bring resolution to troubled areas of the globe. The peace negotiators struggle to reconcile opposing factions. Their task grows tougher each day. They are constantly seeking answers. Are there any?

In April 1992, six hundred people went on a prayer walk of reconciliation from St Paul's Cathedral, London to the Branden-burg Gate in Berlin. When two men, N.J. 'Mac' McCarthy and Charles Simpson heard about it quite separately, they decided to go too.

Mac MacCarthy had flown over thirty missions to Germany and the occupied countries of Europe during the Second World War. As well as military targets, his brief was to carpet-bomb civilian cities. Four of the raids were on Berlin. At the time, he rationalised his actions. His own parents had been bombed out, and it seemed necessary to win the war.

After the war, he met a German prisoner in a village shop. Mac was still in uniform and the prisoner asked him in a broken English accent,

'You bomber?'

'Yes,' Mac replied.

'You bomb Essen?'

'Yes, three times,' Mac replied.

Tears came to the man's eyes. 'I live in Essen,' he said.

Mac was touched very deeply, and that meeting started him on a path to seek reconciliation with those he had once bombed.

In 1971 Mac became a Christian, following a heart attack and subsequent divine healing. In the autumn of 1991 he felt God say two things to him – that he should seek reconciliation and go to Berlin. He did not know how he was to do these two things until he heard about the Prayer Walk of Reconciliation to be held in April of the following year.

Charles Simpson's story was completely different. His ship was blown up by the Germans during the war and he lost many friends and colleagues. He was one of the survivors. Many years later he realised that, as a Christian, he could no longer hold onto any grievance or prejudice. He realised that because of what Jesus did at the cross, unforgiveness is the biggest sin to hang on to. On his 78th birthday he started the 820-mile walk to Berlin with Mac and six hundred others.

Along the way the organisers held 'prayer concerts' at various towns and in the different countries. At each concert the purpose of the walk was spelled out. On many occasions, Mac and

Charles shared the reasons that they were there. Mac was seeking forgiveness. Charles had come to forgive.

At the end of each evening the audience was invited to respond. At one particular church in Germany, several hundred people attended. As people were invited to respond, they thought that only a few of the older people might come up. In fact the whole church got up and came forward! Many were saying how relieved they were that forgiveness was possible after all the time that had elapsed.

The final rally at the Brandenberg Gate, to quote Mac, was, 'Totally crazy. I don't know how many Germans I hugged and kissed that day. It was wonderful.'

If both of these stories could be repeated all over the world then reconciliation would surely come. Maybe revival would follow. Many people still hold onto bitterness and unforgiveness towards old enemies. This is particularly true of the victims of the two world wars. Some who were not even born then have taken on board the hatred from their forebears. The rise of neo-Nazism is only one example.

A new generation is arising, however, who are not prepared to just 'paper over the cracks' and 'let bygones be bygones'. This is a generation of people who have met One who has had mercy on them when they did not deserve it. He forgave them and released them from every debt of the past. They are now setting their hearts to do to others what has been done to them.

Will you join them?

Chapter 15

Questions I Am Asked Frequently

Question: I made my list, prayed through it by myself, but still feel angry when I think of certain people and issues. Why?

Answer: Your anger may still be there because there are debts you have missed. It is possible to pray through these kinds of issues by yourself once you have cleared the more serious offences. I think, however, that it is advisable to have someone with you when you initially go through your list. There are good reasons not to go it alone.

We all have blind spots. Often we do not see the debts fully because:

- we have rationalised, minimised or dismissed them;
- our anger, resentment and distorted thinking have pushed them way back in our emotions;
- unconsciously we do not want to face the pain that confronting those issues would cause;
- we have entered into a subtle form of deception as a result of years of denial;
- shame has locked us up into believing that we are at fault.

God has placed each of us in a body of believers because we need each other.

> *'But now God has placed the members, each one of them, in the body, just as He desired.'* (1 Corinthians 12:18)

Pain and shame will try to stop us, but an unwillingness to work through forgiveness issues with someone else may only be highlighting our independence and self-suffiency – things we need to repent of! Having someone we trust with us to encourage us and pray for us will also give them the opportunity to help us see things we might have missed. Scripture says:

'Bear one another's burdens, and thereby fulfill the law of Christ.'
(Galatians 6:2)

Question: My list is so long, it will take me ages to work through it. Can't I just get some prayer at the end of a meeting and get it 'cut off'?

Answer: If only it were that simple! Many Christians have tried that approach and found it just doesn't work. The powerful prayer from the man of God, binding this and cutting off that, may sound impressive, but when reality hits on Monday morning things may be no different. The question also reveals that in our 'instant' society, Christians can fall prey to the 'quick fix' syndrome: 'I want healing and I want it now!' The Lord is not our slave to do our bidding at our convenience. The opposite is true. Forgiveness is about debt cancellation. If you have not fully realised what the debts are, how can you cancel them?

Many years ago I was asked by a church member who was in serious financial debt to go and help him. 'Before I come,' I said, 'get every bill and invoice ready so that we can see what we are looking at.' On the night I arrived, I took a good friend, Paul, who was a financial 'whiz kid'. The man had got out piles of paper, which were unpaid bills, loan agreements etc.

'Is this everything?' I asked.

'Everything,' he replied. The total was over £9,000.

'What is that behind the clock on the mantelpiece?' I queried. A piece of paper was removed which turned out to be a bill for a pager. 'What's in that drawer?' I enquired. The man pulled out some more bills that he had tucked away at the back of the drawer – hoping they would go away! 'We'll come back when you have found everything,' I said. 'Not even Paul, with all his expertise, can help you if we don't know the full extent of the debts.'

We returned several days later to find that the total debt was actually several thousand pounds greater than the previous figure. The 'everything' we had been told several days earlier was far short of reality. It was only when the full extent of the man's debt was known that my friend could help him with a plan to become debt free.

Hurrying though forgiveness issues often means we miss things and then think that forgiving and releasing does not work. When we are starting to work through painful issues, it is important we do not hurry.

What would you think of a surgeon who hurried an operation on you to remove a cancer, only to leave some of it inside you? Wouldn't you want him to take more time and be more thorough? Unforgiveness is emotional cancer. Determine that you will be thorough in your debt identification and cancellation. If God does an instant miracle in healing your emotions, great. But if not (and that means it will take some time) be prepared for it.

Question: I honestly believe I have forgiven, but I still feel emotional pain. Why?

Answer: Just imagine that I collide with someone as I am leaving a room and as they are entering it. I fall down and crack my head open on the edge of the door. This is not only excruciatingly painful, but also blood is starting to pour down my face. The person apologises profusely and asks for my forgiveness as they help me to my feet. I assure them that it was an accident and that I do forgive them. Despite what I said, they can see I am in pain and again apologise and ask for forgiveness. I reassure them that they are not to blame and that I happily forgive and release them. Despite my forgiveness, I am still in pain and now need healing. Healing is not always instant. I may be able to stick a band aid on my head by myself, but if I have to go to the hospital to have stitches, I need someone else to do that. This is another reason to have someone with you when you are working through emotionally painful issues.

Different kinds of pain

Suppose you have nagging low-level back pain as a result of an old injury. You don't want to take painkillers, so you just live with it. It might score three out of ten on your pain meter. One day you develop a bad toothache. This scores an eight on your pain meter. It is a similar kind of pain but different and has different effects on you physically to the back pain. Another day you cut your hand on a sharp kitchen knife. This pain feels completely different. It needs handling and healing in a different way to either the pain of your back or your tooth. Your backache may make you sit in a certain way. Your toothache may make you eat on one side of your mouth. The cut on your hand may make you wary of sharp blades for a while. They are all painful in different ways.

Pain is a good thing – even though it hurts! It tells us something is wrong and where it is wrong. It's no good putting a band aid on a healthy hand because you have toothache. Emotional pain is similar. It is there to tell us something is wrong, but we had better understand what is causing it or we may 'treat' the symptoms and not the cause.

We understand this in a positive sense in that we can easily distinguish the difference between the feelings of love and of joy. You can experience joy without feeling 'in love' even though feeling in love may well bring you feelings of joy! However, if you do not understand the difference, you may believe that you will only ever feel joy if you are in love. This is just not true!

Sometimes the pain we feel after we have forgiven is not the pain of the original offence. It is the pain of the grief associated with the loss caused by the offence. The grief may be over the loss of the relationship or something else. If, when I fell down, I did not just break my head, but I broke irreparably a pocket watch that had special meaning for me, I might 'mourn' its loss. However, I don't feel 'owed' by the person who I tripped over or demand they pay me back. But I am sad that it is gone and if I feel strong regret, I may need to forgive myself and go to the Lord who binds up the broken hearts.

Most people, if not all, have relationships that go wrong at times. I have certainly experienced this. Sometimes it has been my fault and sometimes it has not. I have had to forgive and release and repent of my bitterness and anger. With some people I have been reconciled and with others I have not. Even with some with whom I have been reconciled, circumstances have changed and I now have a different relationship with them. I have had to grieve the loss of the closeness of their friendship. The 'loss' pain I felt was different to the pain that I felt from the initial break up of the relationship. The Lord is a great healer and has healed me and removed the pain. I am now happy and resolved with the new status of those relationships.

The Holy Spirit is called the comforter and it is He that 'comforts those who mourn' (Matthew 5:4). If your pain is coming from your sense of loss, you need to know that grieving is a process not an event. As you work through the pain, the Holy Spirit will come alongside to comfort and heal you.

Question: How can you expect someone who has suffered a major personal trauma, like the murder of a family member, to immediately forgive the perpetrator?

Answer: I would be surprised if anyone could immediately forgive in such circumstances. If they did claim to, I would question whether the reality of what had happened had fully sunk in. Unless we have been through similar circumstances we cannot really imagine the plethora of emotions someone would go through: shock, horror, disbelief, anger, sadness, grief and fear to name a few. Initially, the emotional need for justice would shout louder on the inside than the need to forgive. As we have seen, it would be far healthier to express those emotions than to shove them down inside.

Since we understand that forgiveness is to do with debts, how can a person really begin to forgive until they start to fully comprehend what those debts are? I cannot imagine Jesus walking up to someone who had suffered such a tragedy and demanding that they forgive there and then. Legalistic Christians may want to push the fact that we should not let the sun go down on our anger. However, it may be a long time before it is possible to fully connect with the complexitiy of emotions and start the forgiving process. It is the unwillingness to forgive that puts us in the torture chamber, not the inability because of a need to come to terms with the trauma.

Harvey Thomas was the public relations coordinator for Margaret Thatcher's government. On 12th October 1984 he was lying in bed on the top floor of the Grand Hotel in Brighton when an IRA bomb went off six feet beneath him. Hurled through the hotel roof, he then fell three stories and got caught on a girder. Ten tons of rubble crashed around him as he lay there for two-and-a-half hours. Unable to move anything except his left foot – which had a nail through it – and with gallons of ice-cold water pouring over him from burst tanks, he was in no doubt that he would die. Miraculously, he survived with only cuts and bruises and was back at work within hours. Five people died and thirty-four others were injured in the attack. Going back to work immediately helped him deal with the trauma and bereavement.

The experience reaffirmed his Christian faith but, he said, 'It was 12 years before I could persuade myself to forgive the bomber Patrick Magee.' Thomas wrote to Magee in prison in 1998 and revealed his identity. Then he wrote: 'I forgive you as Christ has forgiven us.' He says that once he forgave Magee, he immediately felt free of the anger he had carried for years. 'Forgiveness may not be deserved, but it is the only way out of bitterness.'

Question: I can forgive others, it's myself I can't forgive. Why not?

Answer: I have read a lot about the need to forgive ourselves. Many Christian teachers, secular psychiatrists and psychologists, as well as New Age gurus, recommend the practice of forgiving ourselves. A close friend of mine says that forgiving himself was a key to him breaking through into freedom from some past issues. Clearly, forgiving himself 'worked'.

There doesn't appear to be any clear example from Scripture of anyone who forgave themselves. When we read Psalm 51, which is David's cry of repentance to God for his sin with Bathsheba, his perspective on his offence is this:

> *'Against You, You only, I have sinned*
> *And done what is evil in Your sight.'*   (Psalm 51:4)

In fact, we know that his sin was not just against the Lord but against Bathsheba, against Uriah, against Joab and against himself.

> *'Flee immorality. Every other sin that a man commits is outside the body, but the immoral man sins against his own body.'*
> (1 Corinthians 6:18)

Yet we do not hear David forgiving himself.

Peter, one of Jesus' closest friends, went out and wept bitterly when he heard the cock crow. We don't have any evidence that he forgave himself. The apostle Paul considered himself 'chief among sinners' yet throughout his epistles we never get the impression that he needed to forgive himself, even if he did! If God has forgiven us, why would we need to forgive ourselves? Jesus did not say that if our eye offends us, we should forgive it. He had a more radical solution! That is what repentance is.

The greatest expression of love that God could give to fallen humanity was the gift of forgiveness. This was realised through the death and resurrection of Jesus. To forgive is to love. We are commanded to love our neighbour as ourselves. Implicit in that statement is the assumption that we do love ourselves (but not in a self-centred way!). If we love ourselves, then when necessary, we should be prepared to forgive ourselves.

Many people who feel the need to forgive themselves are usually looking to resolve some deep feelings of guilt or shame within themselves. This may be the case even when they know that those they have offended have forgiven them, God included. Very few people feel the need to forgive themselves for minor things, so why the need for what they would consider large offences? Shame and self-rejection make people feel like this. Even though they may believe God has forgiven them, their emotions still tell them they are worthless.

Guilt and shame are different emotions. Guilt is a healthy response that tells us we have violated God's moral standards. Shame is an unhealthy emotion that tells us we are no good – a failure. Shame says, 'I'm a mistake.' Guilt says, 'I made a mistake.' Guilt is removed through the receiving of forgiveness.

Feelings of shame are usually based on a system of perfection- ism. Often shame is embedded in our thinking and emotions by demanding parents, teachers or some other authority figure. We now reinforce those feelings on ourselves by our own 'thought police'. When we fail to meet our own high standards of good- ness or behaviour, we judge ourselves and so feel ashamed and angry at ourselves. In reality, this is false shame which comes from false expectations. We may need to forgive those who put such a yoke on us, and ask God's forgiveness for holding onto such unreal and false expectations of ourselves. We may also need to repent of the pride that made us feel that we were 'above' the sin we fell into!

One powerful aspect of shame is that it isolates us. We feel exposed and inferior to other people. We feel that there is no way of repairing the damage done and so we alienate ourselves. As we cut ourselves off from those who can help, we feel more isolated, more discouragement and more shame. Self-doubt and feelings of powerlessness can grip us when infact this is the time we need others the most.

The body of Christ is called to be a healing community. In rejecting others' help, we are often rejecting the very means of grace and healing that God is offering. A friend of mine recently asked an interesting question. Did I reckon God would withhold the grace of 'feeling forgiven' to make us get together with other people? Good question. I do know from the men's and women's meetings I have spoken at with my wife that many men and women only get freedom from shame when they have openly confessed their sins in front of their friends. Look at these scriptures:

> *'but we have renounced the things hidden because of shame, not walking in craftiness ... '* (2 Corinthians 4:2)

> *'Therefore, confess your sins to one another, and pray for one another so that you may be healed.'* (James 5:16)

> *'Do not participate in the unfruitful deeds of darkness, but instead even expose them;'* (Ephesians 5:11)

Far from feeling rejected, participants at men's and women's meetings have felt the overwhelming sense of acceptance from the rest of the body through prayer and encouragement. This has often resulted in them accepting and forgiving themselves and 'feeling' the forgiveness of God.

When people forgive themselves I think they are connecting with and fully accepting and agreeing with God's forgiveness of them. They are telling themselves that they no longer have to 'pay'; the continual 'beating themselves up' can stop and they finally find they have permission to walk free from the prison they have built for themselves.

If you are continually beating yourself up over a mistake you made, confront the shame and do yourself a favour – forgive yourself!

Question: Do I need to forgive God? I feel He has let me down and disappointed me. He doesn't seem to do for me what He does for others and I am offended with Him.

Answer: If we need to forgive God, do we also need to forgive the devil and the demons that have constantly wreaked havoc in our lives? I don't think so! The context of forgiveness in Scripture is that God has forgiven us and we must now forgive others. The basis for His forgiveness of us is in the atonement made for our sins by Jesus. How can we make atonement for God's sins if He is sinless?!

Often our disappointment with God is there because we have had false expectations and wrong attitudes towards Him. We may be disillusioned with Him, but that is because we were under an illusion – a false perception of reality. As a friend of mine says, 'being disillusioned is good. It exposes our illusions and brings us back to reality.'

Sometimes the church is to blame here because of unbalanced or unhelpful teaching. Promises that your life will be free from trouble if you only ... (fill in the blanks) can only make God seem like a slot machine in the sky. 'I did this, so God must do this,' is a recipe for disillusionment. 'Where was God when I was abused?' may be the angry cry of a hurting person, but their understanding of God's interaction in this sinful world is not a biblical one. Sadly, their pain and their anger may shut themselves off from the very grace that can enable them to forgive and be healed.

If we are disappointed or bitter and angry at God, forgiving Him is not the answer – our heartfelt repentance is!

Chapter 16

Forgiveness Works!

Forgiving and releasing is not a new psychological technique. It is not a formula. It is doing what Jesus told us to do. Having been forgiven and released by God ourselves, we then forgive and release others.

Forgiving and releasing is *settling accounts*. Some of those accounts may go back a long way. For some, therefore, this may be a long process. For others, not so long. Often it is like peeling layers off an onion. You finish one layer and another begins! Having started the process though, it is worth pressing through to the end. Don't give up. Don't feel this will never end. God will give you grace.

It is not just those who have had an unhappy or unstable family background that need to forgive. We have all sinned and have all been sinned against. That is why Jesus came into the world. If we all *need* forgiveness, then we all *need* to forgive.

If the thought of forgiving those who owe you seems daunting, take courage from the following stories. None of them are celebrity status testimonies. That's the reason they are included. We can so easily feel that we need to be a super-sinner rather than just an ordinary Christian to need to experience any kind of 'inner' healing. This just isn't the case. They are ordinary people sharing how forgiveness has changed their lives. If being forgiven by God changed has you, so will forgiving others. Forgiveness works!

Robbed of self-confidence

One evening God reminded me of an incident that happened when I was fifteen years old. Four other girls and I used to do everything together. Then Paula, the 'leader of the pack', began to date Kevin. I told her that he was no good for 'us', as he was into drugs, sex etc.

The next day I received a letter from the others informing me of *all* my faults. These ranged from having bad breath to my bras being too big; from Brad never did kiss me (he wouldn't go near me with a barge-pole) to I needed to see a psychologist.

I took the letter home and showed it to my mother. Her response was, 'Your sister and I were talking the other day and *we* think you need a psychologist too'! My dad's response was, 'I told you Paula was a two-faced bitch.' All I had wanted was some encouragement, but I didn't get any.

That evening I remonstrated to God, 'But I have forgiven them.' He replied, 'Yes but you haven't released them.' I thought for a moment and asked, 'What do they owe me?' 'They owe you twenty years of self-confidence and self-esteem,' He replied.

I welled up with the deepest sense of being owed. It was incredible. Then I was flooded with emotion and an awareness of the injustice and unrighteousness. I also knew that what they had taken from me they could never pay back or restore. I knew I felt owed. I prayed and released them and was then over-whelmed with a personal sense of release. It was wonderful! Now I know that I am released from the effect of having no self-confidence and no self-esteem. Glory to God!

Robbed of a husband

Five weeks after my wedding day I discovered that my husband was having an affair. I was devastated and in the days that followed, my feelings towards the girl became increasingly violent. I was full of anger and hate towards her. During the next fortnight my husband decided to make an effort to mend our marriage. He returned home, but the damage had been done. I never trusted him again, and this incident along with others finally resulted in our divorce.

My feelings of hate towards my husband's girlfriend continued to smoulder and eat away at my heart. Each time I passed her house I radiated hostility towards it! Each time I saw her in town, my hatred would boil up on the inside and I would find swear words directed at her involuntarily coming to my lips. I would have to cross the road to avoid looking at her. I felt that I could have so easily hit her.

This situation continued for some years. During this time, I felt like I had been turned over to the jailers to be tortured as a result of my unforgiveness. I knew that Jesus' command is to forgive others. But it was not until the poison inside me reached an unbearable intensity one day that I realised that forgiving this girl (impossible though it seemed) was my only option. It had to be done and needed determination and self-discipline on my part.

I first prayed for God's help, then forgave the girl and released her from robbing me of my husband. Within minutes of praying and forgiving I felt a great peace flooding into me and replacing the turmoil. I could hardly believe that this inner change was so real. I could hardly wait to bump into this girl in town to see how I would react towards her. I knew that it would be then that I would know whether my heart had really changed.

In fact I did not see her for 2–3 months, but the peace remained and I was able to drive past her house quite comfortably. Then I met her in the supermarket! There we were, advancing inescapably towards each other up the aisle, trolleys laden, with no way out. To my amazement and with no forethought and no effort on my part, I found myself walking up to her with a smile on my face! I greeted her warmly and inside I felt like I was giving her a hug. God's love inside me just overflowed outwards towards her. I am not sure which one of us was most surprised.

A while later, we met again in similar circumstances and again I found myself greeting her warmly. This time, however, I asked her forgiveness for all the hurtful things I had said to her at the time of the affair. This just seemed to complete the healing that God was doing within me. God really honoured my decision to obey His Word. The part I played in forgiving and releasing was so small compared with what He did. In taking away all my hatred and replacing it with His love and warmth, I became a different person.

Robbed of a father's approval

The love from my parents was always implied but rarely physical in terms of hugs and kisses. This, coupled with the sentiments of 'big boys don't cry' and 'be a man' had a detrimental effect on my emotional development. What was really being said was 'don't show your emotions at any cost'.

My father frequently put his work before my achievements. Having spent sixteen weeks going through the Metropolitan Police Training School, I passed all my exams and became a police constable. He didn't even turn up for my passing-out parade. The event became a non-event for me.

Something that helped me understand how I got hurt, and the process of forgiving and releasing, is the analogy of an elastic band held at both ends and twisted until knots have appeared. The twisting represents the hurts, let downs and build up of inner tension over the years. It follows that a reverse process has to take place in order for the person to get back to normality both emotionally and spiritually. Speaking out, 'I forgive you' sometimes isn't enough. We can all make mental decisions to say things that can be quite independent of how our hearts feel. When the heart is involved, more is needed. It is the release part. For me, this came when I hugged my parents for the first time. I knew when I had done this that I had released them. The look on their faces was wonderful!

I am now really aware that whenever my elastic band starts to get wound up, I can forgive and release and be free.

Robbed of adulthood

Talking with a friend one day, I realised that I had grown up physically, but not emotionally and mentally. I had spent the whole of my adolescence believing I was evil and that nobody, not even God, loved me. Also, I believed that I had to look after myself because nobody else would. That I could only trust myself and nobody else. That at no cost could I let go of the hurt emotions inside of me. I could not accept the womanhood that God had given me, because I couldn't let go of the childhood I'd never had.

As my friend and I started to pray, I found I couldn't pray. Then the emotion started to pour out. All the pain, all the hurt, all the injustice. I didn't want to forgive, I didn't want to let go, I didn't want to cancel the debt. I wanted back what I was owed.

I felt wrecked. I knew that all the tears and cries were the cries of the hurt child still within me. Gradually the crying subsided. As I prayed, I forgave and cancelled the debt I felt each person owed me. I accepted the fact that I couldn't go back to my childhood again, and gave it to God. In a 'picture', I saw the struggle, the pain and the crying child recede away from me. I knew that my childhood had finally been laid to rest.

I was so exhausted after this experience that I went home and fell asleep. When I awoke I was overcome by joy at the fact that God had totally changed my life! I was not the person I had been in the morning. I felt a completely different person. No longer a child, but a woman ... the woman God wanted me to be.

Forgiving yourself

When I was in my early twenties, I had an abortion. The trauma was so great that I took an overdose of tablets and was admitted to hospital. Over the following years, although I knew I had done something terribly wrong, I didn't let my conscience get the better of me. I squashed down inside me the pain and guilt I felt. I also got married, had a child and got divorced.

What I hadn't bargained for was that my guilt and the inability to forgive myself started showing in other ways. For no apparent reason, I developed a number of chronic ailments. I started eating compulsively when I wasn't hungry. I developed an overwhelming fear of getting cancer and dying, and losing my children in the same way. I felt condemned, and different to everyone else. I started to see myself as a totally worthless person. More worrying to me than that was that I felt as if something inside me was dead. It felt like a sort of blank space where something important ought to be.

I carried these things with me for a long time. When I became a Christian, friends started to pray with me and showed me how to forgive and release all the people in my life who had hurt me. Although this had a good effect on me, I still wasn't free from the negative feelings and felt separated from God.

One day a friend of mine said that she sensed that I felt a very great need to be punished for something I had done. Her words shook me to the core and I immediately burst into tears – most unusual for me! I knew instantly what the issue was, and all the pain and guilt came to the surface. I had never forgiven myself. I knew I ought to, but felt that what I had done was so terrible that I could not let Jesus bear it for me. I felt I deserved the punishment myself. For two weeks I cried – gut wrenching sobs as I repented and faced up to what I had done and how I had grieved God.

As I prayed again with friends, someone showed me that although God had forgiven me, I had never received His forgiveness for this issue. Then I found the key that unlocked the door for me. I didn't have to ask Jesus to take my punishment, He had already taken it, 2,000 years ago. He carried my sorrows and my pains so that I don't have to. With relief I was able to say the words I needed to say – that I forgave and released myself.

I was unprepared for what happened next. I had a clear picture of a mocking, demonic figure standing between me and God. It was a spirit of death that had had me in its grip for years. No wonder I felt dead inside. It was reluctant to leave, but was banished after a struggle. I then felt a great tingling in my arms and hands, and found myself kneeling down, head on the floor with my hands outstretched. I then received what felt like a torrent of gold dust being poured into my hands. It was a cleansing and refining process, a precious outpouring of God's forgiveness that I was now able to receive. I was reminded of the words of Psalm 24 that I could now 'ascend the hill of the Lord' with 'clean hands and a pure heart'.

The next week of my life was incredible. The fear of death relating to me and my family had gone. The feelings of unworthiness were replaced by a sense of being arrayed in shining gold. The pain that had been within had just melted away. The sense of condemnation left me as did the deadness inside. I felt as if I had woken up after a long sleep! I also found that I could easily forgive others as I had received God's forgiveness for myself.

A problem with men

My dad had a drink problem when I was a child. This meant my early days were full of promises made when sober, but broken when he was drunk. I grew up learning to distrust him. Both my parents told me that 'big girls don't cry', and that as I was the eldest I should set an example. I can remember running to my bedroom and forcing myself not to cry when I was hurt. I even spoke to myself in the mirror saying I hated myself for crying.

Another example of when I felt I hated myself were the times after my dad smacked me for doing wrong. He would go on about it for weeks. Nothing I could say or do would help. It was then that I thought I must be horrible and unlovable as he was always right. Things got so bad that after one incident where he told someone else in the family about something I had done, I carved, 'I hate my dad' in the stairs. I didn't care if he found it because he could then smack me again and I felt I deserved it as I was so horrible. I would always struggle and strive to please people and earn their acceptance.

When I was fourteen a man tried to rape me. This reinforced my negative view of men. I later married a man who turned out to be so much like my dad that I panicked and fought him. This finally ended our often very violent marriage. My whole experience of men had been of violence, frustration and fear. I would do almost anything to keep the peace and ended up a 'doormat' as a result. I would even get panic attacks and leave trolleys full of shopping in the supermarket.

The only time I received attention when I was young was when I was ill. So I made myself sick and ill to get attention. When my marriage broke up, I felt so guilty and such a failure that I became ill and needed major surgery. My life was a mess!

When I became a Christian, my life changed, but not everything was sorted out straight away. I understood about forgiving, but did not understand about releasing. I 'forgave' all the people I could think of because I knew it was what God wanted. It was sometime later, though, that I understood the wonderful truth of forgiving and releasing.

It has taken me months to work through the issues of forgiveness in my past, but God has done many wonderful things in my life over those months. I have been healed from a cyst in the womb as well as heartburn and indigestion which I had had for years. My relationship with my new husband has grown into something I could never have imagined. We are so much closer. I can trust him now, not because he's different, but because God has changed me. I really feel I can be me now ... it really doesn't matter if I get things wrong. I have seen God's love in a new way.

Sucker for a lost cause

After being a Christian for more than two years, I found myself in quite a 'dry' phase. The Lord was still working in many areas of my life, but emotionally I was in turmoil. Someone suggested that I was spending too much time with men, having them round at my house all the time. I was rather offended but prayed and asked the Lord to show me if this was right. I was starting to feel very touchy and was near to tears quite a lot for no particular reason. I asked some Christian friends to pray with me. I assumed that it was tied up with my two failed marriages, but it wasn't. The problem went much further back than that.

When we started praying, the Lord took me back to times in my childhood where I had had to tell 'white' lies. This was because my father had wanted me to cover up some problem at home that 'no-one need know about'. Also, at other times, I was given the responsibility of looking after my sisters, running the home, etc. My father would command that things be done in a certain way. I felt that whatever I did was never good enough as he constantly criticised me and what I did. I forgave and released my dad for all the times he had done this and for the debt I felt owed by him for failing to say the words 'I love you'.

I forgave my brother too. I realised that he had hurt me as well. He was always making horrible comments about me when I was younger. I was called 'fatty', 'tubs' or 'blubber'. It may have seemed like northern humour at the time, but it had hurt me deeply.

I had always felt guilty. Silly though it may sound, I would confess to things that I hadn't done. This went back to my childhood and early teens. My brother would never admit to breaking things. My parents would make us stand and constantly question and shout until one of us admitted to the 'crime'. Because I couldn't stand the bad feelings that went with this, I would 'own up' just to keep the peace. I prayed and forgave my parents and my brother. The release from my guilty emotions was amazing. The hardest one of all, however, was yet to come.

I had always idolised my mother for being the 'rock' in our family. Whenever everything seemed to fall apart, Mum was there, always available. My parents' marriage was awful for years and years, but my mum kept a brave face. Although my father was not physically violent, he was harsh and cruel with his words. He would come and go as he pleased with no respect for my mum. Even after he left her for the fifth time, she still had him back. Then in my early teens 'he' decided to move from one end of the country to the other, taking the family with him and leaving me. I wasn't consulted at all. As a result I felt that I had lost my mum and my two little sisters who I'd spent years looking after. My mum just let it happen.

As my friends prayed with me I realised that my mum wasn't so perfect after all. I forgave her and let the Lord come and heal those areas. I now realise that this had affected the whole of my adult life. I had picked totally unsuitable partners and had surrounded myself with male friends because I was trying to earn some sort of standing with them. I had always been a 'sucker for a lost cause'. As the Lord brought healing into my heart I felt quite different.

I still want to help 'lost causes' now, but for God rather than in order to feel useful. I know that I'm no longer a 'soft option' for others to lean on. Over the last six months the Lord has helped me build some really good friendships with other women in the church. I also realise that the change has to be active on my part – not passive. I have managed to break with people I knew were using me.

I'm happy now to take time with the Lord – I was a Martha not a Mary. I know there are still things God wants to change, but now feel I'm well on the way. After years of feeling bad about myself and wanting to look like or be like others, I actually like being me. It's amazing!

Hope of approval disappointed

I was brought up in a reasonably normal home background. My dad was a teacher and so had long holidays with us. He was great fun and was always making something for us out of odd and ends. I remember how, when getting home from school, he would give us a big hug and a kiss. He was a great encourager and tried to bring out the best in us.

As he was a sports teacher, we would often go to watch him referee for the school team on a Saturday morning. He was also a football league referee. This meant that on Saturday afternoons he would often be officiating at a league game somewhere. This was always exciting and occasionally we got to meet a famous player. During the game I would keep quiet, especially when the supporters started swearing at the ref!

As I got older I developed my own interests that were not sporty at all. In my early teens I became a Christian. At that time, three things became really important to me – music, electronics and my place in the church. My dad wasn't 'into' any of these things. Because I had experienced so much approval and encouragement in my younger years, I expected it to continue in the same way in my teen years.

It was not that he disapproved of my interests, but his almost neutral state made me feel like he did. Rationally, these three areas were out of his own experience. I assumed that he didn't know 'how' to encourage me in them. However, I did feel hurt when he would make really positive comments to me about my brothers' achievements, and seemingly little about my own.

In a time of prayer God showed me that as a result of this lack of approval in my teens, I had sought approval elsewhere. Even in my twenties anyone who looked remotely like a 'father figure' became a potential source of approval and appreciation for me. This was not good news for them, though. They couldn't give me what I was really looking for. The more I tried to get it, the more I felt discouraged and disapproved of! God showed me that I needed to forgive and release my dad for the times that I had expected and needed his approval in my teens and didn't get it. It was a fairly painful experience. I had to ask God's forgiveness for seeking that approval elsewhere when I could have got it from Him.

Since then, I have felt free from the need to be approved of by my dad. If it comes it's a bonus! If it doesn't, I know that I have now found true security in a relationship with my heavenly Father.

Zero emotions

I was brought up in an unhappy family setting. My dad gave me no physical affection, vocal encouragement or approval. There was little or no communication between members of our family and certainly none on an emotional level. This background shaped my character and was to a create fertile environment for later issues.

I became a Christian in my early teens and although this gave me a relationship with God, it did nothing for my underlying needs. Consequently I spent much of my teenage years searching for affection and affirmation in a series of relationships with girls.

I found it very difficult to share about myself on anything but a superficial level. I had no role model. This caused major problems in my subsequent marriage and role as a father. I did not know how to give of myself or share my feelings. I dealt with everything on a logical, mental basis, neatly packaging away issues rather than dealing with them emotionally.

When I got baptised in the Holy Spirit there was a great change in my character but my emotions were still shut down in certain areas. I was unable to be hurt or to feel pain emotionally for myself. Of course I did not recognise that anything was wrong. This is just how I was – my normal self, or so I thought. I even counted being able to package things away as one of my strengths. How wrong I was.

God began to highlight the problems I had in my marriage, so I sought help. It was during a time of ministry that God showed me that the problems lay in a relationship I had experienced in my mid-teens. She was my first love, the only person I had ever opened myself up to. I vividly remembered one particular day. Everything now flooded back. I was there again. This girl had told me that she wanted to break up. I cried and cried until there were no more tears. I was deeply hurt and from that point my emotion died; after that I was not able to be open with anyone again.

The reality that she had screwed up seventeen years of my life, leaving me emotionally dead, needed sorting. I prayed, forgiving her for hurting me, for breaking my trust and destroying my openness. I released her from every debt she owed me.

Following ministry in which the emotional and mental strong-holds were smashed down, I found that my emotions began to function. This was very difficult for me, I felt so vulnerable. Things people said and did began to hurt me. These were normal emotional responses for most people, but they were unfamiliar to me. Many other areas from the past were also opened up. Emotions from times when I should have been hurt but was unable to feel the pain began to surface.

There were particular problem areas in my marriage which surfaced. This made me feel very insecure and hurt. God helped us to talk openly about the issues, which was very difficult at first. We were then able to forgive and release each other. This has brought a freedom in my emotions and my marriage that I did not think possible, a whole new level of communication has developed.

Forgiving and releasing has opened up many areas which have been difficult to cope with and to handle but it has been the key to unlocking many closed areas of my life.

Church forgiveness

Our church didn't exactly split. We had been through some tough times and a number of influential people within decided to leave and join a new church starting nearby. The problem was that over the next year a continuous stream of people followed them. It might have been easier if they had all left in one go. One of our leaders joked, 'We are the fastest growing church in the area – growing smaller, that is!'

Some people wanted to carry on their relationships with me as before, but I was so hurt I couldn't do this. I felt betrayed, not only for myself but also for the leaders and other members of the church. We were never sure who was going to be the next to go. It felt to me that some of the most committed people had just become consumers and now wanted the 'latest brand' of church.

Of course, the grass looked greener on the other side. These people had a new sense of vision and purpose whereas our church was licking its wounds and wondering at times whether it would survive. Those who left had the joy of new relationships and new challenges whereas we felt gutted at the loss of both. It's not that some of the relationships didn't continue, more that they didn't have the same sense of life and purpose they once had.

There was a sense in which members of our church all felt owed in different ways. We were grateful for songs like 'Find Me In The River' by Martin Smith. They helped us corporately express our sorrow and sense of dependence on God. As a church we knew that we could not allow ourselves to become bitter and speak judgements against those who had left, but neither could we just carry on with 'business as usual'. The leaders helped us work through the pain of what had happened, giving us time to meet with God, to forgive where necessary and to receive His healing. They encouraged us to keep good attitudes, which at times was very difficult. They themselves had to work through the pain of what had happened and were open about their disappointments and their pain, allowing us also to minister to them.

What were some of the perceived offenses? Betrayal was a big one. Some people had not even talked through the possibility let alone the probability of them leaving. They just made a uni-lateral decision to go. One week they were a committed part of the body, the next they were committed elsewhere. In one instance, someone on a Monday said something that implied they were with us to the end. On the following Friday they announced, 'This is the end'! We felt owed some sort of discussion, as you would expect friends to have over such a big decision.

Some who had responsibilities just dropped them and left. A large number of the people who had left were also faithful givers. Their faithful giving moved from one church to another with seemingly very little thought of the implications for the church's financial commitments. Church finances became incredibly tight and those who had been supported looked at the possibility of having to get other paid work.

When I heard what some of the people were doing in the new setting, I felt owed. They had been 'brought through' in our church and we were not getting the benefit! What a cheek! However, rather than forgiving them, God showed me that I had to repent of my jealous attitude and that I should bless the expansion of His kingdom wherever that is. Ouch!

I'm sure that some who left had their own forgiveness issues to work through after they had gone. They probably needed to forgive us for our less-than-generous attitude when they left! For us, the need to forgive and release was on two levels. We as individuals had to work through our own sense of the debts we felt owed, but as a church we also had to do the same thing corporately. For example it was no good feeling owed financial support by those who left – they had to be forgiven and released!

Through it all, the leaders kept encouraging us to forgive, release and bless, believing that even though the enemy had meant it for evil, God meant it for good. We were not only praying for the blessing of those individuals but also for the blessing of the new church – that was the real miracle.

Although our church looks very different now, we have seen the blessing and healing of God touch us corporately and individually. We no longer feel 'owed' the people who left. The Lord has multiplied His blessing over us so that although we are smaller in numbers, we have seen an even greater practical outworking of our vision. We have also run joint events with the other church and seen God's blessing on them.

Appendix A

How to Become a Christian

There are many different ways of explaining how to become a Christian. However, the New Testament presents three specific commands to those who want to enter into a relationship with God.

1. Repent!

We read in chapter 5 that Jesus was anointed and commissioned to:

> '... PREACH THE GOSPEL ...
> PROCLAIM RELEASE TO THE CAPTIVES ...
> TO SET FREE THOSE WHO ARE OPPRESSED ...
> TO PROCLAIM THE FAVORABLE YEAR OF THE LORD.' (Luke 4:18–19)

When Jesus began to preach He said,

> 'Repent, for the kingdom of heaven is at hand.' (Matthew 4:17)

In Acts 2, the Jews' response to hearing that Jesus was Lord was to call out, 'What shall we do?' Peter's reply was,

> 'Repent ...' (Acts 2:38)

To repent means 'to have a radical change in attitude towards God and sin'. A person must be ruthlessly honest about their sin before God. Repentance is a determined turning away from wrong. It is not an 'optional extra' when becoming a Christian; it is a command to be obeyed. It is also the first component of a solid foundation for a person's spiritual life (Hebrews 6:1).

2. Believe

Having been confronted by God's power shaking his prison, Paul's jailer asked,

> ' "Sirs, what must I do to be saved?" They said, "Believe in the Lord Jesus, and you will be saved ..." '   (Acts 16:30–31)

The apostle Paul said,

> 'Now I make known to you, brethren, the gospel which I preached to you, which also you received, in which also you stand, by which also you are saved, if you hold fast the word which I preached to you, unless you believed in vain.'
>
> For I delivered to you as of first importance what I also received, that Christ died for our sins according to the Scriptures, and that He was buried, and that He was raised on the third day according to the Scriptures.'   (1 Corinthians 15:1–4)

What was it the jailer had to believe?

> '... that Christ died for our sins according to the Scriptures, and that He was buried, and that He was raised on the third day ...'
>   (1 Corinthians 15:3–4)

To believe, the jailer had to turn to God and put his faith in Jesus and make Him Lord (that means 'Boss'). He had to believe that Jesus died for him personally. Jesus bore the punishment of the whole world's sin, when He died on the cross.

> '... Christ was sacrificed once to take away the sins of many people; and he will appear a second time, not to bear sin, but to bring salvation to those who are waiting for him.'
>   (Hebrews 9:28 NIV)

A person must not only believe that Jesus died for them, but that He rose again from the dead.

> '... if you confess with your mouth Jesus as Lord, and believe in your heart that God raised Him from the dead, you will be saved;

> *for with the heart a person believes, resulting in righteousness, and with the mouth he confesses, resulting in salvation.'*
>
> (Romans 10:9–10)

3. Be baptised

> *'Peter said to them, "Repent, and each of you be baptized in the name of Jesus Christ for the forgiveness of your sins."'*
>
> (Acts 2:38)

Some time later, Peter preached the gospel to non-Jews. Look what happened as he preached:

> *'"Of Him all the prophets bear witness that through His name everyone who believes in Him receives forgiveness of sins."*
>
> *While Peter was still speaking these words, the Holy Spirit fell upon all those who were listening to the message.*
>
> *All the circumcised believers who came with Peter were amazed, because the gift of the Holy Spirit had been poured out on the Gentiles also.*
>
> *For they were hearing them speaking with tongues and exalting God. Then Peter answered,*
>
> *"Surely no one can refuse the water for these to be baptized who have received the Holy Spirit just as we did, can he?" And he ordered them to be baptized in the name of Jesus Christ ... '*
>
> (Acts 10:43–48)

Peter did not give them the option of being baptised in water 'if they felt ready'. He saw evidence of their repentance and faith in that the Holy Spirit had been poured out on them. He ordered them to be baptised. This was in obedience to Jesus' command to His disciples in Matthew:

> *'And Jesus came up and spoke to them, saying, "All authority has been given to Me in heaven and on earth. Go therefore and make disciples of all the nations, baptizing them in the name of the Father and the Son and the Holy Spirit, teaching them to observe all that I commanded you; and lo, I am with you always, even to the end of the age."'*   (Matthew 28:18–20)

The word 'baptise' means 'to dip, immerse or submerge'. Figuratively, it means 'to overwhelm'.

'As they went along the road they came to some water; and the eunuch said, "Look! Water! What prevents me from being baptized?"

And he ordered the chariot to stop; and they both went down into the water, Philip as well as the eunuch; and he baptized him.

When they came up out of the water, the Spirit of the Lord snatched Philip away; and the eunuch no longer saw him, but went on his way rejoicing.'   (Acts 8:36, 38–39)

When Philip the evangelist preached Jesus to the Ethiopian eunuch, he must have told the Ethiopian that the correct response was to be baptised. Notice that they both went down into the water. The Greek scholar, W.E. Vine says, 'baptism is the process of immersion, submergence and emergence.' Baptism is the correct biblical response for those who have repented and believed.

If you want to become a Christian, you must:

- repent of your sin
- believe in the Lord Jesus

and in response to Jesus' command,

- be baptised in water.

You will certainly need help getting baptised. Here is a prayer that you could pray by yourself right now, if you want to express your repentance and faith in Jesus.

'Lord Jesus, I know I have sinned and I am truly sorry. I repent and turn from living my own way. I turn my life over to You. Thank You that You died on the cross for me and were punished for my sin. Please forgive me for my sin and cleanse me from it. Release me from the debts I owe You. Come into my life and take control as my Lord. As You have forgiven and released me, I will forgive and release those who have offended me.'

In the Acts 1, Jesus spoke about the Holy Spirit:

'... for John baptized with water, but you shall be baptized with the Holy Spirit not many days from now.'   (Acts 1:5)

Later, He says,

> '... *but you shall receive power when the Holy Spirit has come upon you; and you shall be My witnesses both in Jerusalem, and in all Judea and Samaria, and even to the remotest part of the earth.*' (Acts 1:8)

The Holy Spirit came upon the disciples on the Day of Pentecost.

> '*When the day of Pentecost had come, they were all together in one place.*
>
> *And suddenly there came from heaven a noise like a violent, rushing wind, and it filled the whole house where they were sitting.*
>
> *And there appeared to them tongues as of fire distributing themselves, and they rested on each one of them.*
>
> *And they were all filled with the Holy Spirit and began to speak with other tongues, as the Spirit was giving them utterance.*' (Acts 2:1–4)

Remember Acts 10? The Holy Spirit was poured out there also. The 'believers' also spoke with tongues. God has not changed! He is still pouring out the Holy Spirit on those who believe. Look what Peter said in Acts 2:

> '*Repent, and each of you be baptized in the name of Jesus Christ for the forgiveness of your sins; and you will receive the gift of the Holy Spirit. For the promise is for you and your children, and for all who are far off, as many as the Lord our God will call to Himself.*' (Acts 2:38–39)

You are part of the 'all who are far off' that Peter was talking about. Therefore the promise of the Holy Spirit is for you too. You can be baptised in the Holy Spirit in the same way as the believers in Acts 2 and Acts 10 were. Do you remember that the word 'baptise' figuratively means to overwhelm? To be baptised in the Holy Spirit means to be overwhelmed by the Holy Spirit. You can open yourself up to God the Holy Spirit right now. Ask Him to come and fill your life.

Talk to someone you know who is a committed Christian. They should be able to help you further.

If you have a story of forgiveness that you would like to share with me, please email it to forgiveness@visionofthefuture.org.uk – I would love to hear from you.

Appendix B

Visual Aids
to Sharing Forgiveness

If you have found this book helpful, you may want to copy the
following pictures and keep them in your Bible. When you come
to share with someone about forgiveness, they can be a useful
visual aid.

1. Root, Fruit, Seed and Soil

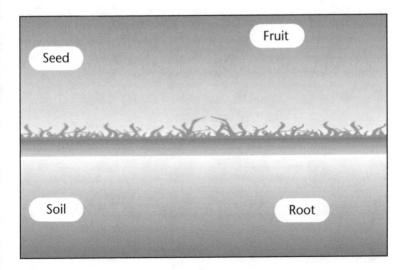

2. The Soil of Insecurity

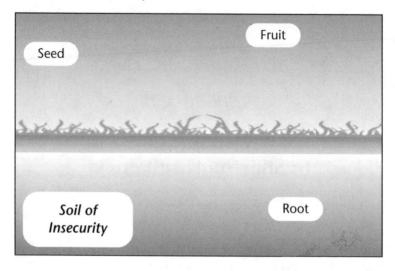

Resulting from a lack of: *acceptance; affirmation; appreciation; affection; encouragement;* and *love.*

3. The Seed of Offence

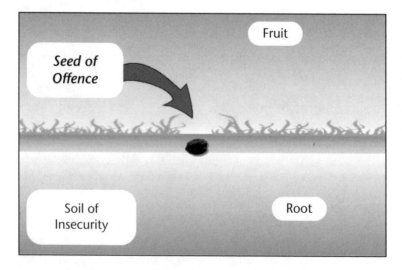

Resulting from: *what others said; what others didn't say; what others did; what others didn't do.*

4. The Root of Bitterness

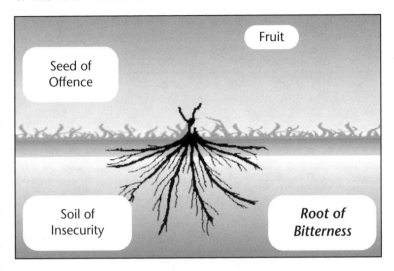

Resulting from: *what you think; what you feel.*

5. The Fruit of Resentment

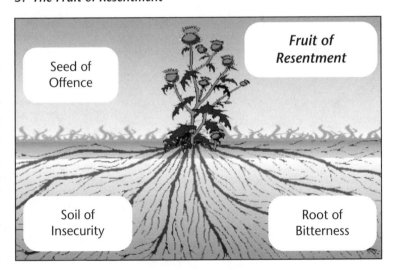

Resulting from: *what you say; what you do.*

If you have enjoyed this book and would like to help us to send a copy of it and many other titles to needy pastors in the **Third World**, please write for further information or send your gift to:

Sovereign World Trust
PO Box 777, Tonbridge
Kent TN11 0ZS
United Kingdom

or to the **'Sovereign World'** distributor in your country.

Visit our website at **www.sovereign-world.org**
for a full range of Sovereign World books.